Saint Thérèse de Jésus, Henry Edward Manning

Jesus in The Host and in The Priesthood

chapters extracted from the life of the Reverend Mother St. Teresa of Jesus, abbess

of the Covenant of Poor Clares, at Lavaur

Saint Thérèse de Jésus, Henry Edward Manning

Jesus in The Host and in The Priesthood
chapters extracted from the life of the Reverend Mother St. Teresa of Jesus, abbess of the Covenant of Poor Clares, at Lavaur

ISBN/EAN: 9783337332600

Printed in Europe, USA, Canada, Australia, Japan

Cover: Foto ©Lupo / pixelio.de

More available books at **www.hansebooks.com**

JESUS IN THE HOST AND IN THE PRIESTHOOD

CHAPTERS EXTRACTED FROM THE LIFE OF THE
REVEREND MOTHER ST. TERESA OF JESUS,
ABBESS OF THE CONVENT OF POOR
CLARES, AT LAVAUR

WITH A PREFACE

BY

THE CARDINAL ARCHBISHOP OF WESTMINSTER

LONDON: BURNS & OATES, Limited
NEW YORK: CATHOLIC PUBLICATION SOCIETY CO.
1888

PROTESTATION.

URBAN VIII., on the 13th March, 1625, issued in the Sacred Congregation of the Inquisition a decree, confirmed afterwards on 5th June, 1634, prohibiting the publication of books by any authors departed this life in odour of sanctity or martyrdom, containing their acts, miracles, or revelations as coming from God, without the recognition of the Ordinary. Whatsoever, then, is found in the following pages, even though published in French with the *imprimatur* of the Ordinary, is here republished in English as having no divine authority of the Church, but only such authority as is human.

NOTE.

THE Contemplations on the Priesthood, here offered for the meditation of priests, are extracts from the life of a holy and humble Abbess of Poor Clares, who died March 26, 1884, in the odour of sanctity, at Lavaur.

The Reverend Mother, St. Teresa, who was born January 2, 1828, wrote, by order of her directors, her wonderful life. She had, especially during her last years, most exalted Contemplations on the Priesthood. From these, necessarily abridged in the history of her life,* it has been thought useful to draw up this selection.

* *Vie de la Reverende Mère Sainte Thérèse de Jesus, Abbesse du Monastère de Sainte Claire de Lavaur.* Ecrite par elle-même, mise en ordre par M. l'Abbé Roques, archiprête de Lavaur. 3ᵉ edit. 2 vol. Privat, Toulouse.

PREFACE.

WHEN I first read the *Vues sur le Sacerdoce* of Mother Teresa of Jesus, the intense truth, piety, and beauty of her thoughts made me desire to put the book into the hands of our priests. I therefore requested F. Police of the Marist Congregation to translate it into English. He has kindly done so very accurately.

The book had been examined and published in the Diocese of Toulouse, under the authority of the Ordinary, and I therefore could not doubt that it could be traversed *inoffenso pede*.

From time to time, as I reflected on the book, I began to doubt, not of the accuracy of its theological outline, but of certain details, chiefly verbal, as for instance where it is said in page 18, line 18, that Our Lord "unites Himself personally to the priest in order by his means to impart to the faithful His own sacramental life". The word *personally* might be misunderstood to mean hypostatically, which would be erroneous, but in any other sense it is capable of a safe and true meaning. In page 20, lines 5 and 6, this is guarded; in page 19, line 8, the parallel of the Incarnation and of the consecration of the priest is described as the same mystery. This might be misunderstood to mean more than analogy; so again in page 21, line 11, it is said that Christ *personally* and *substantially* unites Himself to the priest, clothes him entirely with Himself, so much so that the priest in some sort "*loses his own personality*". It is evident that these terms need to be restrained within their own proper limit. So again in page 22, line 6, it is said that "the greatness and power of the sacerdotal grace cannot be diminished by the personal dispositions of him who receives it". This is certainly true of the *res sacramenti*, but as M. Teresa profusely shows afterwards, she cannot have intended to speak of the *gratiae sacramentales*. She is also probably speaking only of the sacramental actions of the priest, in which, as she says, the priest is a mere instrument, as St. Augustine says, *Petrus baptizat, Christus baptizat.* This is fully and beautifully explained in pages 23 and 24.

In many places the word *substantially* is used with a freedom intelligible, perhaps, in the French language, but with us, being restricted to its philosophical and theological sense, its use may easily suggest an erroneous conception. It would seem to me to be sufficient to put the reader upon his guard by the passages already quoted. The substance of this series of views, or lights, or contemplations on the priesthood is so profoundly true, so intensely fervent in its conception, so elevated and so severely theological, that no considerate reader can be in danger from any imperfection here and there in its terminology.

It has been well said that one of the internal evidences of the truth of the New Testament — especially of the Apostolic Epistles—is to be found in its "unanxious language". Everyone who has had to deal with the controversies of Arians, Unitarians, Sacramentarians, and Calvinists will know how even the inspired writings can be interpreted in erroneous senses, and how true is the axiom of St. Augustine, that no language is sufficiently perfect to express adequately the conception of the mind. There is, however, no doubt that the verbal over-statement of certain passages in these pages is amply balanced by accurate statements in other parts. The equilibrium is thereby restored. But over-statement is always a danger. In the inspired writings there is a calmness and a self-restraint, a measure and proportion which results from "the analogy of faith".* Nevertheless, there are passages of a divine intensity, which some men count to be over-statement, and others explain away. For example—

"That Christ may dwell by faith in your heart; that being rooted and founded in charity, you may be able to comprehend with all the saints what is the breadth and length, and height and depth; to know also the charity of Christ, which surpasseth all knowledge, that you may be filled unto all the fulness of God" (Ephesians iii. 17-19). Here are three expressions which peremptorily refuse the glib hermeneutic "that they only mean this". The indwelling of Christ is not hypostatic, but everything short of it. The knowing that which sur-

* Rom. xii. 6.

passeth all knowledge is nothing less than the *totum non totaliter;* and the being filled unto all the fulness of God can only be understood when we shall know even as we are known.

"The charity of Christ presseth us (*urget nos*), judging this, that if one died for all, then all were dead; and Christ died for all, that they who live may not now live to themselves, but unto Him who died for them and rose again" (2 Cor. v. 14, 15). This is not less than to be *alter Christus*.

"Know ye not that your members are the temple of the Holy Ghost who is in you" (1 Cor. vi. 19). Here is *inhabitatio* in every sense, except hypostatical. Again, "he who is joined to the Lord is one spirit" (*Ibid.* 17). The interpreters whom Aristotle calls "straw-splitters" would surely affirm that this is a hypostatic unity in which the human personality ceases to exist.

"Ye are dead, and your life is hid with Christ in God" (Coloss. iii. 3). This needs no comment to men of sound mind.

"God is Charity; he that abideth in charity abideth in God, and God in him" (1 St. John iv. 16). Here would seem to be the *circumincessio* extended to the creature.

"In that day you shall know that I am in My Father, and you in Me and I in you" (St. John xiv. 20). The Son is consubstantially in the Father: how then are we in Him, and He in us?

"He that heareth you heareth Me" (St. Luke x. 16). St. Augustine says, "*Vox capitis vox corporis*," "*Si in una carne, quomodo non in una voce*". But this identity of voice demands common sense to interpret it.

"With Christ I am nailed to the Cross. And I live, now not I; but Christ liveth in me" (Gal. ii. 19, 20). This unanxious language may be midnight to the wise, but it is noonday to the simple, who live in the divine tradition of the Church. They have "the unction from the Holy One, and know all things" (1 St. John ii. 20).

If these divine realities of union and indwelling and personal co-operation be true of all the faithful, they must be eminently true of the Priest of Jesus Christ, to whom He said, "As the Father hath sent Me, I also send you" (St. John xx. 21).

The analogies of the Incarnation and the Holy Mass: of the office of Mary and of the priest: of the presence of the Word made flesh in the Blessed Sacrament and in the priesthood, are divine realities, in which we are all bound *non plus sapere quam oportet sapere, sed sapere ad sobrietatem* (Rom. xii. 3). Not only in our public teachings as priests, but in our private meditations, we are bound to keep always in mind the divine tradition of the faith in all its precise and luminous distinctions "according to the proportion of faith," or rather, as St. Paul wrote, κατὰ τὴν ἀναλογίαν τῆς πίστεως, "according to the analogy of the proportions of faith" (Rom. xii. 6). Thus much I have said to guard the words of Mother Teresa from any misconception which would have profoundly afflicted her illuminated soul, and also to show how profound and divine are the realities of the supernatural life, as the Holy Ghost describes them in the inspired writings.

HENRY EDWARD,
Cardinal Archbishop.

Octave of the Ascension, 1888.

CONTENTS.

CHAPTER I.
(pp. 1-116).

CONTEMPLATIONS ON THE PRIESTHOOD.

	PAGE
The greatness and dignity of the Priesthood,	5
The power bestowed on it by God,	6
The priest pre-eminently the son of the most Holy Trinity,	7
The most holy Virgin the mother of priests,	10, 58
The grace of the Priesthood and that with which Mary was filled at the moment of the Incarnation,	11
The priest another Christ,	17, 23
Special glory of the Unction of the Priesthood,	18, 20
Union of the priest with Jesus in the Host,	21, 25
Fruitful ministry of the priest,	24
Flaws in the souls of priests,	28, 30, 32, 34, 40, 43, 66, 80, 110, 121
The priest in the world,	31
The priest and Jesus in the Host,	37
Mystery of the life and action of Jesus in the priest,	39
Pride and rashness of the writer,	46
Jesus in the Host and His operations in souls,	48
Life of Jesus in the Host and His life in the Priesthood,	51
Three homes of Incarnate Wisdom,	57
The priest is to Jesus what Jesus is to God,	87
Beauty of the soul of the priest,	93
The priest a living altar of Jesus,	96

CHAPTER II.
(pp. 117-132).

THE ASSOCIATION OF THE PRIESTHOOD.

Its object,	117
What the Sacred Heart of Jesus expects from members of the Association,	120

JESUS IN THE HOST AND IN THE PRIESTHOOD.

Chapter I.

CONTEMPLATIONS ON THE PRIESTHOOD.

August 8, 1879. Yesterday, I was suddenly filled with awe at the sight of the greatness and dignity of the priesthood. I could see that the priest is but an outward appearance behind which is hidden the sacred Person of God the Son, the Word made flesh, to continue His life wholly consecrated to God His Father and to souls.

The priest is another Jesus Christ, and only two loves ought to consume his life and devour his heart: love of the glory of the Most Holy Trinity, because of the relationship which he bears to the Three Adorable Persons; and love of souls, whom God at the moment of his ordination committed to his hands, to be their father, giving him, so to speak, over them a power of life and death.

Here I was, as it were, overpowered by the dependence on His own creature to which Jesus submits Himself, in giving the priest all power not only over His blessed manhood, His sacred Person, and His Eucharistic life, but also over the life which He desires to have in souls, investing him with the power to beget them to grace, and communicate to them with more or less abundance His divine life. It seemed to me that the priest had a great and twofold inheritance to keep and to defend : the first and the greatest is that of the sacred Person of Jesus Christ, over whom he has an almost absolute power. Every day, at the moment of the consecration, this divine inheritance is entrusted to him anew, together with the fulness of the infinite merits of the Man-God, and with an abundant participation of His divine attributes. It is, indeed, into the hands of the priest that Jesus, in becoming a victim, lays the exercise of His own power, and communicates it to him, His minister, by making him its store-house and dispenser. It is, indeed, the word of the priest, which becoming His own, reduces Him to His Eucharistic helplessness. With regard to Himself, Jesus makes the priest the storehouse of the exercise of His divine power, to give him the glory of investing His sacred Person with it anew. This divine privilege is not reserved for the priest alone. All souls are more or less endowed with it, according to God's purpose in them; all have the means to give to Jesus in the Host the free exercise of His power in their own hearts, and can obtain, by their prayer and sufferings, that other souls may render Jesus no longer powerless in the good He desires to do them. In the most sacred Host, Jesus, poor by His own will, stripped of the exercise of His divine power, expects from His poor creature the divine garment which He has so freely and lovingly laid aside. He more especially expects it from His ministers, to whom He has also confided the fulness of divine life, and the source of all light, to be diffused among souls. The priest, to be a faithful guardian of the power of the life and light with which he is entrusted, ought to be constantly united to Jesus, to act only by Him, to live only by Him and for Him, to be enlightened only by the light of this divine Sun of Justice; for, otherwise, what can be His influence over souls? How shall he be to them the dispenser of the power of Jesus if he acts independently of his Divine Master? How shall he be able to communicate spiritual life, with all its efficacy, if he does not himself draw it from its source? How shall he be able to enlighten them, if he be not himself a shining light, always reflecting the light of the life of Christ? How many ministers of the sanctuary, unable to appreciate the inheritance which they have received, let Jesus languish in the poverty and the helplessness to which their word, the organ of the word of God, has reduced our Divine Saviour! Who can give back to Jesus Christ the exercise of His divine power if he to whom it has been lent keeps it buried or himself ignores it? Who shall give to God souls having a perfect life if he, whose duty it is to be their father, communicates to them only a feeble, imperfect life? Who shall enlighten them, if the light which is to guide them has become darkness? I feel unable to express all that has been revealed to me by the interior light.

August 9, 1879. In obedience to the strict obligation imposed on me to say all that which has passed within me, I propose, in spite of all it costs me, to continue the account which I could not finish yesterday.

In all that the light revealed to me concerning the dignity of the priesthood, nothing struck me so much as the immense love of Jesus, which causes Him to strip Himself of His power, in order to bestow on the priest the glory of restoring it to Him. The consideration of a priest who is a faithful guardian and dispenser strikes my soul with awe, by showing him to me invested with a divine grandeur; but at the same time a secret and most painful anguish seizes my heart, in thinking that there are ministers of Jesus in the Host whose life does not correspond to the sublimity of their vocation. They are not bad priests, but they, through their own fault, do not know the divine treasures confided to them. They have charge of them without being themselves possessed of them; and, as a consequence of their neglect in applying themselves to the knowledge of their sublime ministry, let the meek Lamb of God pine alone in the depths of the sacred Tabernacle, where He dwells, poor and stripped of all power to communicate Himself to souls, that are unable to hear His Eucharistic voice, unless a faithful echo repeats it to them.

It seems to me that the priest is eminently the son of the Most Holy Trinity; the Father shares with him His divine paternity, in using his voice in order to give a sacramental being to His Son and to beget souls for Him, by imparting to them divine life.

The Word makes him the instrument and dispenser of His sacred Word, depositing it with him as a hidden treasure, in order that he may unceasingly draw from it for the nourishment of himself and of souls. He gives him full power over His sacred Person, so that the priest possesses both the written word and the living and Eternal Word of the Father.

The Holy Ghost communicates to him the fulness of His gifts and lights, His divine love, in order that he may have the power efficaciously to touch souls, to enlighten them, to guide them safely, to take complete hold of them by divine love, so as to detach them from the earth, to which everything attaches them.

The priest being the well-beloved son of the Most Adorable Trinity, the bosom of God becomes his abode; and as a son delights to dwell in his father's home, thus a priest should never leave either in mind or in heart the bosom of the Most Holy Trinity. He should only come down among men to save them and draw them after him in the love of God who created them.

The light which enlightens me shows to me that Jesus meant this when He said to His Apostles: "As the Father hath sent Me, I also send you". Now, the Father sent His Word and at the same time kept Him in His bosom. The Word was made man, and lived among men, remaining always inseparably united to the Divine Persons and living their divine life. The priest, faithful image of Christ, ought then to imitate Him in His manifestation in our humanity—as He Himself said to His Apostles: "As the Father hath sent Me, I also send you".

It seems to me that the greatest misfortune of the priest is to show himself too much a man, and not to consider himself, as he is indeed, separated from and elevated above the entire creation, and thus bound to have with it none but divine relations. As God has become his inheritance, he also ought to be the inheritance of God, the faithful companion of Jesus in the Blessed Sacrament, the defender of His divine rights, the unwearied propagator of His honour and glory.

The priest will expose himself to neglect these great duties, will lose sight of them, or look upon them in too natural and sometimes interested a light, if he deals frequently with the world, if he comes down too often among the perishable things of earth, which make us lose sight of things invisible; and then, instead of letting the people know and love

Christ in his own person, he exposes himself to contempt, criticism, and even insult.

The sight of this urges me to sacrifice myself, and to pray that God may give none but worthy priests to His holy Church, men penetrated with a true sacerdotal spirit, looking to God only and souls in the exercise of their ministry. I think that in praying for that end, we sympathise with the most bitter sorrows of Jesus in the Host and correspond to His most ardent desires. It is to ask, moreover, in the most direct manner, that the kingdom of the Divine Jesus in the Eucharist may be established in every heart.

January 5, 1880. To-day the interior light has shown to me that if every soul is a spray which ought to blossom with Jesus and to reveal Him unceasingly, the soul of the priest is like a parent branch, around which other branches, more or less numerous, ought to grow and develop. For, though springing from the divine seed, from which they draw their life and the food which sustains them, they nevertheless do not receive the full influx of it, except through the main branch, which draws its sap from the plenitude of the divine seed. I can see of what importance it is for the good of souls, and for the glory of Holy Church, that the priest should be a faithful minister and dispenser of the treasure confided to his care; how he is bound to give profusely what he receives so plentifully, so liberally, and so freely.

I feel myself driven to implore the Immaculate Virgin to obtain for the ministers of her Son Jesus the true spirit of the priesthood; and it appears to me that I see that Mary has received from her Divine Son special grace and mission to form the heart of the priest for the sacred functions of his sublime vocation, and to obtain for him a constant renewing of the grace which maintains and develops the spirit and grace of the priesthood—a grace which, in its essence and in its effects, is closely related to the fulness of grace with which Mary was filled at the moment of the Incarnation.

The interior light showed to me that the grace of the holy order of priesthood gives the priest not only a special grace, a fulness of that grace, but the Author Himself of all grace, the Holy Ghost, who gives Himself personally to the soul of the priest, bringing to him the fulness of all His treasures, giving to him the power to distribute and produce grace in souls and beget them to true life.

As the Holy Ghost came to dwell in Mary Immaculate with the fulness of all His gifts, to produce in her the Sacred Manhood of Jesus, so also does this Spirit of Love unite Himself to the priest to make him His instrument, by means of which he produces the sacred species, the sacramental being put on by Jesus, in order to dwell still amongst men. It seems to me, furthermore, that the holy unction, which marks the soul of the priest with a divine and eternal character, and binds the very essence of his soul to the adorable Person of Jesus, to make him another Christ—that this unction, this consecration, is a participation, and, as it were, an imitation of the consecration made by the Godhead in the Sacred Manhood of Jesus. This consecration elevated the Sacred Manhood to a dignity altogether apart and unique in making it subsist in the very Person of the Word—dedicating and devoting it altogether to be the instrument of the Divine Word, to serve Him in all His works, and reproduce them outside Himself. This consecration constituted the Sacred Manhood as the divine channel of all the workings and outpourings of the Godhead in souls, made Him the mediator, the bond of union between God and the creature; in sum, made of the Manhood and the Person of the Word, through the hypostatic union, one and the same Person.

January 6, 1880. The light of grace draws my soul to the consideration of the same mysteries of love. Yesterday it showed me the effects of the consecration made by the Person of the Word on the Sacred Manhood of Jesus; to-day it reveals to me more clearly, more particularly, the relations of this divine consecration and its effects with the consecration and the effects which the sacred unction of the priesthood works in the soul and the whole person of the ministers of the altar.

This sacred unction is shown to me as marking the soul of the priest with the very seal of the Godhead, uniting it so intimately, and so indissolubly, to the very Person of Christ, that it becomes its living image. By this holy unction, which the Three Persons of the Holy Trinity impress on his soul, and which they confirm by the personal gift of the Spirit of Love, the minister of God receives a consecration which makes the whole of his person the property of Christ by a title that no creature can ever share with him. Separated from all, raised even above angels, the priest becomes the exclusive property of God, the special inheritance of Christ, who invests him with His strength, His power, His divine virtue, to make him the instrument of all His works; so that everything is divine in a priest fulfilling the functions of his sacred ministry.

All he does comes from God, goes back to God, has its growth and ends in God. As the Word in His Incarnation infused His whole self into the Sacred Manhood to deify it both in itself and in its operations, in like manner Jesus infuses His whole self into the soul of His ministers. It is the same mystery of grace and of sanctity which makes of the priest a living sacrament of Jesus Christ.

It is not only in order to make the priest the organ of His word and to give Jesus a sacramental being that the Eternal Father clothes the priest with His divine power, and that the Spirit of Love fills him with the fulness of His graces, and overshadows him with His power; but it is also that he may beget Jesus in souls and give them to God.

An interior light shows to me that this power and this virtue, which constitute the very essence of the grace of the priesthood, are always given to the priest, independently of his personal dispositions, and produce their effects in the functions which he exercises. But the effusion, of the fulness of life and of divine graces, which are given to the priest that he may be able in his turn to give them to souls without losing any of the superabundance which he possesses—this divine effusion I say, which is granted to the priest for himself and for souls, can be checked, narrowed, and limited in its influences, and produce less or greater fruits of grace and of life, according as the priest shows himself a zealous and faithful dispenser. The divine power with which he has been clothed may reveal itself in all the works of the priest, as it may also remain in him like a buried treasure, which produces only weak and insignificant effects, according as he keeps himself more or less united with Him who is the strength, the virtue, and the power itself of the priesthood; in proportion also as he effaces himself and disappears in order that only Jesus Christ may be revealed and allowed to have in him and by him a full and entire liberty of action in souls.

After this vision I felt myself still more strongly drawn than before to pray and ask that the ministers of the Holy Altar may fully understand that the power and fruitfulness of their sacred ministry entirely and supremely depend on their union with the Holy Victim, which they daily offer up; and that there is nothing truly quickening in their works, but only so far as they are done in the Spirit of Jesus and in His own divine love.

It seems to me that prayers for the clergy are those most acceptable to Jesus in the Host, and most comforting to His divine Heart, in alleviating, in some way, one of His greatest afflictions and most incessant solicitudes. For Jesus in the Host sees the priest as he is, that is, as the principle from which the life of souls, the glory of His Immaculate Spouse and of His Eternal Father depend. Because He sees the priest as His love has made him, Jesus in the Host asks His Heavenly Father that His priests may be a source of life, holiness, and glory.

This grace makes me pray also that souls may recognise the grandeur of the priest, have faith in his power, and respect his dignity. The want of faith and respect have been shown to me as great obstacles to the marvellous effects of the divine influence of the priesthood, as a hindrance to the fruits of life which it ought to produce.

January 29, 1880. This grace presses me still more strongly, especially these last few days, to pray unceasingly for priests. In renewing this invitation, it puts before my mind, as by an interior light, the sublimity of the priesthood, and shows to me that there are consecrated souls who have fallen from this divine height.

I would I could express, as I see it in the inward light, the greatness and power of the priest; but I feel that my words cannot explain these things, much less the feelings, which they excite in my heart: as I said just now, I enter somewhat into the meaning of the words: *The priest is another Christ.*

The truth, the reality, of this saying becomes as it were palpable to me, so lively, so deep is the impression that I receive. I see this greatness and this power included, and concentrated in the unction of the priesthood, given to the sacred minister by that same unction which alone makes the priest, by conferring on him sacerdotal grace.

An inward light shows to me that through this sacred unction the priest becomes among all creatures the eldest and well-beloved son of the Holy Trinity, its living tabernacle, or rather, its holy of holies—that it has in him a very special abode, bequeathing to him in some way the essence of Its divine majesty. Through this same unction, the priest enters into most intimate relations with the Three Divine Persons.

The Father clothes him with His power, sharing, in a certain way, with him His title of Paternity, by bestowing on him the power of giving His sacramental being to the Divine Word, whom He begets eternally; and giving, moreover, to him the title of fathership over souls, to beget them to the life of grace, by giving them a new birth in Christ.

The Word gives the priest not only the efficacious virtue of His own word, but Himself, the living and substantial Word of the Father. He unites Himself personally to the priest, in order by his means to impart to the faithful His own sacramental life; in order also to act and work in him and by him. To this end He infuses Himself into him with the plenitude of His divine life, and of His infinite power.

The Spirit of Love overshadows him and

pours into his soul the fulness of His grace, the superabundance of His gifts, that he may give a sacramental existence to the Incarnate Word, to form Jesus Christ in souls, and make Him grow in them in all His fulness. The outpouring of the Holy Ghost and the abundance of His gifts in the soul of the priest, seem to me to be the same mystery of grace and sanctity as that which took place in the Most Holy Virgin at the moment of the Incarnation.

The priest, in order to give to Jesus his sacramental being, to form Him and make Him grow and increase in souls, receives of the same fulness—grace, power, and holiness—as Mary. Thus, because of the special indwelling of the Holy Trinity in the soul of the priest, and of the relationship thence resulting with the Three Divine Persons; on account also of the sacred obligations which are imposed on him of the great and sublime office which he has to fulfil, the priest is anointed by an unction which, as an inward light shows me, is an image of the divine unction of the Sacred Manhood of Jesus.

This same light shows to me, as I am trying to describe it, the connection between these two anointings.

The Sacred Manhood of Jesus is anointed by the Godhead personally, that is, by the hypostatic union of the Word, who unites the Sacred Manhood in one and the same person to Himself.

The sacerdotal unction which the priest receives is the seal which the Godhead, that is to say, the Blessed Trinity, stamps on his inmost soul, whereby its very essence and all his person are consecrated to the Incarnate Word, binding him to Jesus in so special a manner as to make him *another Christ*. The unction of the Godhead consecrates the Manhood of Jesus as its own living temple, the sacred throne whereon the Holy Trinity in Person rests, making this Sacred Manhood to belong wholly and completely to the Word, existing only in Him, by Him, and for Him. In like manner, also, the sacerdotal grace given to the priest by the holy unction consecrates him as a living temple, wherein the Holy Trinity dwells in a very special way; as a throne, whereon reposes the Majesty of the Most High, as a living image which ought to reflect Him, who is the splendour of the eternal glory. His whole being, his soul, especially, becomes the exclusive property of God; bound to live only in Christ, by Christ, and for Christ.

It is not by effusion or participation, it seems to me, that the priest receives the power and virtue of Christ; but that Christ personally and substantially unites Himself to him, clothes him entirely with Himself, so much so that the priest, in some sort, loses his own personality; and that it is Christ alone who acts and works by him, just in the same way as the Divine Word acted and worked by the Sacred Manhood.

Jesus is in the priest, living and acting by him, as by His instrument, working by him, in certain ways independently of him, in others dependently on him—dependently on him as far as the outward action required by the divine operation, the priest being in this respect the instrument, the supplement of Christ; independently of the priest, as to the effects of the work, and of the outward action itself. The priest being nothing but a mere instrument, adds to or takes nothing from the effects of the action and of the operation, which is altogether the work of Jesus. Thus the greatness and power of the sacerdotal grace cannot be diminished by the personal dispositions of him who receives it; nor can the actions which he does in virtue of this grace undergo any modification on account of his personal dispositions. . . .

January 30, 1880. How great does the office of the priest seem to me! No words of mine can explain what my interior light shows me of this greatness. When I endeavour to express the insight which God has given to me, a boundless horizon is opened before the eyes of my soul; and there is such unity, such perfect connection in all that it sees, that, in grasping one truth, it takes hold of all, though in each something special is to be found.

What appears to me to be the essence of the greatness of the priest, the groundwork and very substance of sacerdotal grace, is the sublime and divine union on which Jesus enters with his soul, a union so close and intimate that human language can only repeat, *The priest is another Christ.*

In a certain way, and in the degree of which a creature is capable, all that God has done for the Sacred Manhood He has done likewise for the priest. All that He has given to the former He gives also to the soul of the priest: because, in the sight of the Most Holy Trinity, the priest is a living and continued incarnation of the Incarnate Word. In the priest and by the priest God sees His Christ still living amongst men to perpetuate in their midst His Eternal Priesthood.

I cannot say how possessed I am by the reality of the presence of Jesus in the priest, and by the feelings that I experience thereby! I see that Jesus is present, living, acting and working in the priest and by the priest; and that, from the fact of this personal presence of Christ, the dispositions of the minister have no influence on his acts, as regards their essential value. All that the hand of the priest blesses is blest; all that he consecrates is consecrated; all that he does by virtue of his sacred ministry is worshipful, because it is Jesus alone, who, in him, is the principle of action and operation.

If the effects of his acts do not correspond with the acts themselves, if these effects do not produce all the fruits they ought to do, the reason is, that besides that which is essential in them, the power of which nothing can change or diminish, they have also a something special, which is the outcome of love in him who effects them, and in him who receives them: this work of love is union with Jesus.

It is shown to me that the soul of the priest has two kinds of union with Jesus, making two kinds of indwelling: that of Christ in the priest, and that of the priest in Christ.

The first union, to which corresponds the first indwelling, is that which confers on the soul of the priest sacerdotal grace, which is given, sin notwithstanding, when the priest performs the sacerdotal acts of his sacred ministry. For Jesus is always then present and living in him, in his acts and works, and this by the virtue and the power itself of the priesthood: this union alone suffices to give their essential value to the acts of the priest. But, besides this union and this abode of Jesus in the priest, a union which nothing can break when once made, there is a second union and second indwelling, which are the effects of a twofold love: the love of God for His creature, and the love of the creature for God.

It is, as I understand it, this second union and this second indwelling which, in a definite manner, gives fruitfulness to the acts of priests.

January 31, 1880. I said in my letter of yesterday, that the union of love, between "Jesus in the Host" and the soul of the priest, was shown to me as giving its fruitfulness to the sacred ministry.

This light comes to me from the words of Jesus: "He that abideth in Me, and I in him, bringeth forth much fruit; for without Me you can do nothing".

In these words, which my inward light refers to the priest, my soul discovers the two modes of indwelling and the corresponding modes of union of which I spoke yesterday. I see, above all, that it is absolutely necessary and indispensable to the priest, for the fruitfulness of his ministry, not only to let Jesus live in him, but still more to live himself in Jesus. The priestly unction, which has entirely cut him off from the world and placed him in a state where the things of earth cease to be for him what they are for the rest of mankind—this sacred unction, and the grace which it bestows, have set the priest apart from his own life, from every thing of self, to give him up, to consecrate him exclusively for the guardianship, service, and defence of the Holy Eucharist and for the good of souls.

Henceforth the whole spiritual and natural being of the sacred minister becomes the property of God, who, in return, gives him possession of His Incarnate Word. Jesus has fulness of life in the priest, who also, in his turn, has fulness of life in Jesus ; and this fulness is brought to pass and bestowed by love.

An interior light shows me that the soul of the priest is a channel through which Jesus makes His life, His grace, His light and love flow into souls; a superabundance, which even amounts to fulness, of all these goods, is found in the soul of the priest, that he may be able to bestow, without measure and unceasingly, that which he so freely receives. Jesus Himself is, in the soul of the priest, the source of life, of grace, of light, and of love.

The soul of the priest is again shown to me as a centre in which is gathered all the activity of divine love, so that this love, passing constantly to its source, may be poured out with all its might and power upon souls, to change and to transform them.

It seems to me that divine love naturally follows the more or less immediate, abundant, and efficacious presence that God has in His creatures. There is no creature in which He is more present than in the priest; there is, furthermore, no one in whom the divine love is more powerful and abundant.

The priest receives this love not only for God, but also for souls; and as all the works of God, in proportion as they are loftier and more elevated, are also more perfect, the priest, who ought to love in souls the divine reality which is in them, receives a power of love capable of embracing this reality.

Love is not in the soul of the priest as a simple virtue; it is there undoubtedly, and ought to be there in a supereminent degree; but it is there above all in its source, in its substance, because the Spirit of Love reposes in him with the fulness of His gifts.

His love is therefore Love itself. If he loves souls, it is not with his own heart, but with that of Jesus Himself, who has become his loving power. The heart of the priest ought therefore to be as a source of love, whose life it is always to be flowing, in order to bestow unceasingly on souls the outpouring of divine charity.

Such is his mission. To be faithful to it he ought constantly to seek for souls, to love them, to draw them towards God, in order to make them love Him, and to love Him more in himself by loving Him with them.

But an interior light reveals to me a great flaw or failure in the soul of the priest to correspond with the infinite gift of His divine love which Jesus has made him! . . .

February 1, 1880. I think I finished my letter of yesterday by saying that I see a great failure in the souls of a number of priests to correspond with the love of Jesus, but I do not like to dwell upon the sight or speak of it. But as it strikes the eyes of my soul more and more, and as I am bound to relate all that passes within me, I will describe all that I can of this vision. But, meanwhile, I ought to add to that which I said yesterday, that an interior light shows to me the soul of the priest, as a centre in which Jesus, the Divine Sun of Justice, gathers and condenses the rays of His divine light in a manner so immediate, that this centre becomes itself bright enough to illumine souls by the reflection of the rays which it absorbs.

Thus it is revealed to me that Jesus is in the soul of the priest a spring of life, of light, and of love ; and that the priest is for souls in like manner a spring of life, of light, and of love.

Jesus imparts a share of the fulness of His

divine life to the soul of the priest, and He desires this life to be manifested in the fruitfulness of the souls over which the priest exercises his divine mission.

The fruits of this fertility in the soul of the priest seem to me to be a spirit of separation and total estrangement from the world, a complete effacement of his own life in order that the spirit of the life of Jesus may possess the whole of his being. This spirit and this life are alike the element wherein the consecrated soul must live to arrive at a true priestly holiness.

The light shows to me that this truth, so generally known, is not, however, practically understood by some consecrated souls, because they do not sufficiently realise that their whole life must be summed up in the duties of their sacred ministry, and that the spirit and usages of the world are not to be for them what they are for the rest of Christians.

The first cause of the failure which the light discovers to me in the sacred minister, is the want of that spirit of separation which hinders the priest from keeping himself in mind and heart far enough from the world. Hence follows the weakening of the priestly spirit, and the primary cause of the little fruit produced by his ministry; because, instead of revealing and manifesting the life of Christ, the priest reveals and manifests himself.

A second cause of failure in priestly life which the light shows me, is the want of generous and disinterested zeal. If the love of Jesus is fettered in ordinary souls, wherein He meets with hindrances, it suffers a twofold captivity in the soul of the priest wherein it finds such obstacles. It is not only the love of Jesus which is imprisoned, but Jesus Himself, who is made prisoner in the place where He should have full and perfect liberty; for the soul of the priest is the exclusive property of divine love. It has only been chosen and separated from the world to be used by Him as a faithful instrument, that it may always be in a condition that He may act through it.

Offering up as he does the Lamb of God, the priest ought to be His first victim, by a devotedness without limit and without measure, which should make of him in some sort a martyr of God in the Host.

February 2, 1880. To-day again I feel obliged to come back to the same subject, because grace draws me thither, and an interior light unveils it more clearly to my eyes.

My soul is in great tribulation. I would not resist the grace, nor turn myself from the visions that Jesus bestows on me; at the same time, I desire not to give them more importance and reality than they have in fact. I am possessed by a double fear, which causes me a suffering which I cannot express.

I have tried to turn my mind to other thoughts, but the efforts I make to that end are useless. Attracted by a power which I cannot resist, my soul is always busied with the same contemplations. If I try to withdraw myself from them, I find myself flying back again; and I have peace and rest only in following the leading of grace.

My great cause of sorrow is the sight I have of the feebleness of the priestly spirit in some consecrated souls. This weakness seems to me so great that I fear to be deceived, or that my imagination exaggerates the vision, if it comes from Jesus.

I would like not to believe the revelation of the light, but the intimate conviction of its reality is produced by the light, and falls on my soul with a force which does not allow me to doubt. An interior voice says continually: " Pray, sacrifice thyself unceasingly to obtain from My heart the graces of light and of strength, of which My ministers stand in need ".

To these interior words succeeds a light which shows me chasms great and deep as an abyss, the Eucharistic sorrows which they cause to the Sacred Heart of Jesus, the almost infinite evil which they work in souls.

Words cannot express that vision, nor the pain and suffering which it causes me. It excites, above all, a keen desire of making reparation to Jesus in the Host and of union with Him, to ask, together with Him and by Him, of the Holy Trinity, in the name of His Eucharistic satisfactions, that the true spirit and holiness of the priesthood may be renewed in the priests of Holy Church.

I said yesterday that the second cause of the failure of the priestly life seems to me to be the absence of zeal.

My interior light insists more and more on this cause. It shows me that the unquenchable zeal which ought to make of the priest a true martyr of the God whom he daily offers up, is found by Jesus in few only of His ministers. In some it is soiled, tainted, if not entirely destroyed, by the spirit of egotism, by self-interest; and our dear Lord finds Himself a prisoner in shameful bondage. His divine charity, which had made the heart of the priest a channel to convey to souls the divine outpourings of His love—this infinite charity finds itself cramped and straitened in the narrow prison of a heart shrivelled by selfishness.

The great, the sublime end which Jesus had in view in separating the priest from the rest of Christians was to dedicate him completely and totally to His divine love, to use him always, and in all things, as an instrument, in the same way as His Sacred Manhood has been dedicated to the Word, to serve Him in the accomplishment of His divine ends.

The office and the function of the priest, as regards Jesus in the Host, seem to me like those of the Sacred Manhood towards the Divine Word ; as the Word was in the Sacred Manhood the cause or spring of the action, which was of Him, came from Him, returned to Him, as nevertheless He needed the Sacred Manhood to use It as an instrument in the execution of His adorable designs, in the same way Jesus in the Host stands in need of the priest to do His work for souls.

February 3, 1880. The attraction that grace exercises on me becomes more and more strong and powerful. My soul cannot resist it : I find it always in all things praying in union with Jesus in the Host for Holy Church.

My interior light shows me only Jesus in the Host in His relations with the priest; and again, the relations of the priest with Him.

It seems to me that the intimacy of these

relations forms a union so great that actually Jesus in the Host and the priest make but one whole; whose parts, though distinct, are neither separated nor separable. A saying of mine the other day reveals to me in the clearest and most concise manner all the uniformity and harmony, the intimacy and union of the priest with Jesus, and with Jesus in the Host; for I seem to understand that the priesthood has been instituted only for the Eucharist in itself, and for the Eucharist as regards souls. Listen to the saying, which is a light to my soul : *The priest is a living and constant incarnation of Jesus.*

It seems to me that this is the true point of view in which the character of the priesthood ought to be considered to grasp all its greatness, its dignity, and its sacred obligations; and also to understand the dependence —full of mercy and of love—of Jesus on the priest ; and the equally great dependence the priest ought to have on Jesus.

In the Incarnation the Eternal Word became incarnate in order to render Himself in some way visible. He united Himself with the Sacred Manhood for no other end but to make it serve as an instrument of His actions, in order to make it the subject of all His divine works, and to execute in it and by it the Eternal decrees.

In like manner, in marking the priest with a sacred and divine character, in identifying Himself with him by the grace of the priesthood, the intention of Jesus is no other than by his means to render Himself visible to souls; to make him serve as an instrument in order to execute His designs of love and of mercy on souls; to continue in him and by him the great work of the Redemption and sanctification of the elect. Jesus in the Host is, therefore, in reality, as present, as living in the soul of the priest, who is according to His own Heart, as the Divine Word is present and living in the Sacred Manhood.

This union of the priest with Christ is the most real and most perfect outcome there could be of the hypostatic union: it is this real similitude which makes of the priest the masterpiece of the power and of the love of God— a sacred rod, whose flower is God Himself.

Jesus in the Host dwells in the priest, continuing by him the execution of His designs on souls. In all these designs everything is definitely the work of Jesus. There are works which His love alone can accomplish; and He does them without receiving any help from the instrument which He has united to Himself. There are other works, however, which Jesus, in His Eucharistic state, will not, and can not, perform without the aid of the priest, who is the external agent of His love.

If Jesus remains absolutely independent of His minister, as regards the interior operations of His grace in souls, if He has not intended therein to abdicate His divine power, so that only the soul to whom grace is given can, by its dispositions, paralyse the effects of that grace, and render powerless the omnipotence of Jesus, yet it is nevertheless true that in the works which require external action, the effects of which depend in a secondary manner upon such action, Jesus has made Himself absolutely dependent on the priest, who acts towards His Sacred Person as the supplement of His Sacred Manhood. If this action fails, if this secondary cause of the Grace does not answer to the Grace itself, it comes to pass that the primary cause—that is to say, the action of Jesus Himself—does not reach the soul for whom it was intended, or exercises very little influence over it; for Jesus stands in need somehow of the power of action which the priest has to lend Him.

In this point of view, how fettered and enslaved does Jesus seem to me!

February 4, 1880. How little known and understood by souls, and by many of those who are its privileged recipients, is the mystery of faith and love of Jesus present, living and acting in the priest.

Hearken to what the light reveals to my soul. If Jesus is not known and understood in His Eucharistic life, He is still less so in the life that He lives in the priest, and by the priest; and it is because the sacred minister does not seek to penetrate into this great mystery of love and divine power, because he does not sufficiently understand how totally and absolutely dependent he is on Jesus, and how much Jesus desires to be subject to him, that this sweet Master finds Himself so often reduced to the most shameful and most sorrowful slavery and captivity, in that very dwelling in which His Sacred Heart ought to have full and entire liberty, where He would find His full power of action.

This morning it seemed to me that I heard an interior voice say to my soul: "The living sanctuary that Jesus in the Host has chosen among men for His personal abode, this holy sanctuary is soiled by the spirit of the world, which is continually thrusting itself therein, under every form; the purity of this consecrated place is dimmed, the holy of holies is profaned, by worldliness and self-seeking.

"The Sacred Heart of Jesus in the Host is deeply wounded in His love by His very love, by that love which He pours with a divine liberality into the souls of His ministers, which the infidelity of many casts back upon Him, in the shape of keen and burning arrows, which wound and pierce His adorable Heart; which the neglect of many more throws back upon His divine Heart, like an ocean of sorrow, brimming with the bitterness of their ingratitude. Almighty God finds Himself captive and prisoner in the bonds of those whom He had chosen to be His bosom friends: who only show themselves such when their zeal turns to their personal advantage: who cease to be the defenders of the cause of God when the struggle needs self-sacrifice."

A light shows to me that the true apostolic spirit, which is essentially a spirit of entire self-sacrifice, of martyrdom, is rare; and that Jesus does not find it in all His ministers, because they are not thoroughly convinced that, being bosom friends of Him who has chosen them, they are also, and above all, His servants, His martyrs.

I seem to understand, indeed, that the priest is by office and by duty the martyr of God in the Blessed Sacrament; and that the blood, which he ought to shed every day on his altar, is his labour, his self-denial, his strength, his life itself, pouring it out, drop by drop, in the work of his holy ministry. But, unhappily, Jesus does not find in every priestly soul this devotedness, this ardent zeal! . . .

It is shown me that in some ministers of the altar this pure zeal, this divine charity, is found corrupted by the spirit of self-interest; they either neglect the sacred duties of their ministry, or mix with them too much of themselves, forgetting that they are only instruments and servants; and that to serve faithfully they ought to efface themselves, and let Jesus alone be seen in them.

It seems to me that our dear Lord suffers (in much and the same way) from these two defects of devotedness — from these two failures of true zeal for the glory of God, and the salvation of souls.

The one of these defects He sees renders almost useless, or, at least, deprives of much of their fruit, the tender and loving devices by which His divine charity endeavours to gain souls, to draw them to knowledge and love of Himself. By the other, which causes no less damage and loss to souls—which, perhaps, more effectually estranges them from Him—He sees Himself delivered and exposed to the contempt, the criticism, the insults of the world.

I cannot express all the evil which the interior light shows me as the outcome of these failures of zeal in the priest, nor the bitter sorrows which they inflict on the Sacred Heart of Jesus in the Host!

February 5, 1880. To-day I come back again to the same subject, constrained in some way by grace, and that because I had not said all that the interior light revealed to me.

In spite of the repugnance and difficulty I experience in so doing, I feel that I must not omit anything; that this light is like a blessing which God imparts through my soul as He would through any other channel; but that this gift does not belong to me in any way whatever, and that I must keep back nothing.

This light reveals to me that there are in Holy Church priests who do not live according to their divine vocation, who do not seriously fulfil its duties, who are not thoroughly impressed with the sacredness of their obligations; that such ministers of the altar dishonour the sacred character with which they are invested, by the neglect, the want of devotedness, and spirit of self-interest which, in some cases, seem to have taken the place of the apostolic spirit, which is the very essence of the priesthood.

It seems to me that the greatest evil does not altogether come from bad priests, terrible as it is in its havoc among souls, and still more terrible in the sorrows which it causes to Jesus in the Host; yet the great wound, more difficult to cure than any other, more hideous than all in its deadly effects on souls, is the weakening of the priestly spirit, the want of true and disinterested devotedness, the want of purity of zeal in some of the clergy.

Though they are not bad, yet in them and by them the sublime and divine dignity of the priesthood is made like to the spirit of the world, by compromises and connivances between the priestly spirit, which is the true Spirit of Jesus, and the spirit of the world, which is its most irreconcilable and bitter enemy.

Thus degraded, the dignity of the priesthood loses its power and ascendence over souls. Hence follows, in the living sanctuary of Jesus in the Host, a sort of subtle and sacrilegious traffic, oftentimes hidden under such appearances of good as deceive even the culprits themselves.

But, though concealed, these unworthy dealings nevertheless produce poisonous fruits, so that in the most sacred duties, which should be done only with the most pure intention for the glory of God and the salvation of souls, there steals in the seeking of personal interest, self-esteem and self-satisfaction. Thus the house of prayer is found to be profaned.

The soul of the priest seems to me to be the holy house in which the praise of the Most Holy Trinity should always be heard : because the priest is by office and by duty the angel of prayer, who ought to be always carrying the prayers of the faithful to the altar of the Lamb, our Victim. He ought to be prayer personified, a living prayer, to fill up what is wanting in that of souls.

February 6, 1880. I feel in the depths

beneath my soul a tempest of temptations raging against me, showing what pride and rashness possess me, ignorant and miserable woman that I am—only able to garble truth—to write these things.

These temptations, moreover, show me that since it is my desire to employ my time for the glory of God, it would tend more to that glory were I to betake myself to prayer for the multitude of souls who are going to perdition, rather than to busy myself with the reform of clergy, who are not bad.

This last temptation, however, has no hold on me, because the interior light clearly shows me the weakening of the priestly spirit, the deep abyss of evils caused thereby to souls, the bitterness of the sorrows inflicted on Jesus in the Host, that it would be impossible for me not to believe the truth of what is shown me.

This same light reveals to me that prayer for the clergy means not only the priest, but that in him, and by him, it embraces the generality of souls; that to pray for the priest is to work directly and most quickly for the good of Holy Church; that it is to serve her most gloriously, in obtaining that which is her true and only glory, viz., saintly and valiant apostles, devoted and zealous pastors, brilliant and shining lights.

Thus I see, in that interior light, that to pray for the priest is to console Jesus in the Host in His sharpest sorrow, and to sweeten the most bitter of His Eucharistic sufferings.

To impress this truth more clearly on my mind, an interior voice, furthermore, seemed to say to me: "When one wishes to save a little child, who seems to be already in the grasp of death, is not the best way to restore it to life and to preserve its powers undiminished, to entrust it to the care of a mother, who will surround its tender years with that lavish care and delicate nurture of which only a mother's heart has the secret, the skill to carry out?" "It is the same," adds this interior voice, "in an infinitely greater way, with the priest and the souls of men. He is to them, indeed, what the mother is to her babe." The same God who has concentrated in the mother's heart all the strength and devotion of natural love has also given to the heart of the priest all the strength and devotion of supernatural love; or rather, He who is infinite and essential Charity has poured out Himself into the soul of the priest, in order that the priest may take hold of souls with an embrace of love, and love them with the same love as that with which God loves them, with the Heart of Jesus Himself.

February 7, 1880. Grace made use of the words with which I ended my letter of yesterday to recall me once more to the subject of which I was speaking, viz., the need Jesus in the Host has of the priest's action to do His work in souls.

I will therefore try to speak of it again. I do not know, however, whether it is in the same way that the interior light reveals to me the necessary co-operation of the priestly action. Should it be so, I can only say what it pleases Jesus to show me day by day.

In His infinite mercy, Jesus in the Host has deigned to-day to reveal to my soul that, hidden in His Holy Tabernacle, He is ever busied in strongly drawing souls to know Him and to love Him by the sweetness and the might of His grace; that to Him alone it belongs to move them with His divine attractions, to gain them by the outpourings of His divine goodness; but that, in order to reach by His grace the souls that live far from Him, to reveal to them His hidden attractions, Jesus in the Host stands in need of a channel, of an instrument of action.

The priest discharges both functions. His vocation itself makes him the regular means by which Jesus works in souls. His sublime mission is to go and meet the soul who wishes to come, to prepare the way for the love of Christ. He is like a strong arm with which Jesus embraces and presses souls to His loving Heart, to raise them up together with Himself to the bosom of the Father in a divine and unspeakable union.

It is not that Jesus limits His power of action to the priesthood alone, or that He uses no other means, no other instruments to act and work in souls; but all active power—all grace so to work—flows from the supreme power which God has bestowed in all its fulness in the priesthood alone.

All grace flows from this divine and first fountain as the stream from its source, and must return to it again; because all power and all grace come from Christ; and the living and present reality of Christ is in the priesthood.

After thus marking the intimate relations of the mysterious life of Jesus in the sacrament of His love, grace recalls me to the consideration of the comparison drawn yesterday in my soul between the priest and souls on one hand, and the mother and child on the other.

Grace fills my mind with a new light on priestly devotedness, showing me still more clearly its sublimity, its indispensable necessity, its unlimited extent.

I see, also, that the absence of this devotion, the imperfection of this divine virtue, is an evil of which Jesus in the Host has most to complain, that which most painfully wounds His Sacred Heart; because it is the beginning and source of all other failures in the priestly life: for where there is no true and constant zeal, there love also is but weak and languid;

nature regains its rights and shows itself with all its passions, since the germ of all its desires and concupiscences is still alive.

The priest is a principle of life for souls; divine love is itself the principle and source of this supernatural life. When, therefore, in the heart of the priest this divine love has lost its perfect and inviolable purity, its fulness of strength and of power, in the spiritual regeneration of the souls he is called to form, instead of implanting in them the life of Christ in all its power and virtue, the priest imparts to souls only a weak and feeble life, a life which more or less reproduces the defects and imperfections of his own life.

February 8, 1880. I understand better than I ever did before how closely and intimately bound together are both the mystery of the life of Jesus in the Host, and the mystery of the life of Jesus in the priesthood. I seem to understand that they form but one and the same mystery, one necessitating the other, mutually perfecting and completing each other, by a perfect development of the life of Christ in souls.

The light reveals to me that the priesthood has been instituted only for the Eucharist; that its duties, its relations with the Man-God, hidden in the sacrament of love, constitute the very essence of this divine vocation, and form the very foundation of its sacred obligations, all the rest of which are dependent and secondary. Thus, before all things and above all things, the priest belongs to Jesus in the Host, and ought to live only for Him. This supreme and divine dependence is his greatest glory, and demands a purity which should keep him always in a state worthy to enter into the Holy of Holies, and to touch with his hands uncreated purity, the Lamb of God slain from the beginning of the world.*

In contemplating Jesus in the Host, it seemed to me that I saw a spring of divine life issuing from His Eucharistic throne, flowing from His Sacred Heart, seeking to pour itself into souls by those legitimate channels which Jesus Himself had chosen, that is, first and principally, by His sacred ministers; and then my soul understood

* Apoc. xiii. 8.

more perfectly what I said yesterday of the supernatural life which the priest ought to impart to souls.

February 9, 1880. The attraction by which the grace draws my soul to pray for the ministers of the sanctuary seems to be redoubled in might and power.

In presence of Jesus in the Host, under His divine eyes, I feel myself always irresistibly drawn to the same subject. This morning I felt a certain affliction, either because I should have wished to think of Jesus alone, or because I was afraid of losing time in this occupation, and giving way to my own imaginations.

Scarcely had this thought entered my mind, even before I had time to dwell on it, when grace reproached me for it as an imperfection, giving me to understand that Jesus may reveal Himself as He pleases, either in Himself or in His consecrated ministers; that we think of Him alone, and love only Him when we do what He wishes, and are satisfied with what His love bestows. Moreover, Jesus in the Host and the priest seem to me so closely and so divinely united, that the eyes of my soul cannot, as it were, see Jesus without immediately discerning the priesthood.

Again, I cannot ask that the mysteries of love in His Eucharistic life should be known by souls, without asking that those of the life of Jesus in the priest should also be known.

The interior light reveals to me that it is in these two ways of dwelling in the midst of His Church, in these two forms of the life He leads therein, that Jesus in the Host wishes and desires to be known, loved, glorified; because, in these two mysteries of faith and of love, He is equally unknown, misunderstood, despised, insulted.

I seem to understand that these two revelations are necessary for the establishment of the Eucharistic reign in souls, so much light does the knowledge of the life of Jesus in the priesthood throw upon the knowledge of the life of Jesus in the Eucharist.

As a consequence of this view, it seems to me that to pray that God may give to His Church worthy and saintly ministers, filled with the true sacerdotal spirit, is to hasten twofold the hour when Jesus in the Host shall be able to manifest and establish His Eucharistic reign in the hearts of men : for the priesthood is the great means, the chief instrument by which Jesus in the Host would be made manifest.

The interior light showed to me that this manifestation of Jesus is the great, the supreme duty which is imposed upon the priest, and that which generally he most neglects ; that this manifestation would be the most efficacious means to draw souls out of the cold selfishness which freezes and kills them, and to restore to them that strength and vigour which they have lost.

February 10, 1880. Jesus has deigned to-day to send me a new ray of His divine light, by which He reveals to me something of what His all-creating power has done in behalf of the soul of the priest.

Jesus makes this light shine from these words, which an interior voice has repeated to me again and again during the day : " Wisdom has built herself a house ".*

* Prov. ix. 1.

It is shown to me that these words have received their full and perfect accomplishment in the Sacred Manhood of Jesus, because it is the divine house built by Uncreated Wisdom, the sacred temple which was not made by the hands of men.

I see that the sense of these words is equally applicable to the Most Holy Virgin; that it is in her, after Jesus, that they have their fulfilment, because she was the house, the living tabernacle wherein the Divine Wisdom chose to become man; and that it was from her immaculate flesh, from her virginal blood, that the Holy of Holies, in which the Incarnate Wisdom dwells, was made. The interior light reveals to me that, after Mary, it is in the soul of the priest that these words are realised in all their truth. The soul of the priest is not only destined, like every other soul, to be the abode of Jesus by grace, to be so in a yet more real manner when Jesus dwells truly and substantially in the soul by Holy Communion; but by an exceptional privilege, reserved only to the priesthood, the soul which is invested with this sacred and divine character enjoys the personal and habitual presence of Jesus, a presence which makes that privileged soul a permanent home of Incarnate Wisdom. . . .

It is revealed to me that the Sacred Manhood, Mary Immaculate, and the soul of the priest are the three living homes wherein Incarnate Wisdom desires personally and permanently to dwell—a dwelling altogether different from that which it takes up in other souls; and though these three abodes seem to me one infinitely above the other, and each of them forms an order apart, yet I think it is always the same mystery, unfolding itself in divers ways and proportions. It is also shown to me that, by reason of this special and personal indwelling, each of these three sacred mansions has been consecrated by a divine and special unction.

The unction received by the Sacred Manhood was the unction itself of the Godhead by the hypostatic union of the Word. The unction received by Mary Immaculate was conferred upon her by the incarnation itself of this Word in her virginal womb; lastly, the priestly unction received by the sacred minister is an expansion, a living and real imitation of the two former unctions; for, as the Sacred Manhood is entirely made over to the Divine Word, and makes with Him one only Person, so the priest, having received the sacred unction, is entirely made over to Jesus to become one with Him; and as Mary gave to the Word His Sacred Manhood, in like manner the priest gives to Jesus His sacramental being.

The interior light shows to me that the Most Holy Virgin is the model priest, ordained by Jesus Himself to serve as an example to the soul of every priest, as having received from her well-beloved and Divine Son Jesus grace and special mission to form them for the great and sublime obligations of their divine ministry, and to communicate to them the true spirit of their holy vocation.

It is shown to me that the soul of the priest, in its filial devotion towards Mary, ought, above all, to love, honour, imitate, and glorify three of the titles of this Immaculate Mother, which it shares with her in some degree:

viz., her title of priest and sacrificer, her title of divine motherhood, and that of her immaculate purity.

Each time that grace constrains me to pray for Holy Church, I feel that I must have recourse to the intercession of Mary. The light shows to me that the heart of this tender Mother burns with an immense love, a most ardent zeal for priestly souls, on account of the ties which bind them to Jesus, and that her prayer in their behalf is omnipotent.

February 11, 1880. The light, which enlightens my soul, reveals to me that, in forming the soul of the priest, Uncreated Wisdom, intending to make it her special abiding place, is not satisfied with giving it ample and sublime endowments in view of the divine vocation for which that soul is destined, but she bestows on it a special capacity to receive the grace of the priesthood ; she endows it with particular aptitudes for these great virtues which belong to the essence of the priesthood ; her divine hand bountifully adorns it with every gift, in order that her divine perfection may be seen therein almost substantially as in a mirror.

All these great and marvellous gifts which Almighty Power bestows on the soul of the priest are like the pillars of the living temple in which Christ is to dwell; they are, as it were, the seal of the divine election and the first benediction which redeeming grace sheds upon the house that Divine Wisdom has built for herself, until the grace of the priesthood crowns the building with the divine gifts.

It is shown to me that the holy unction does not bestow upon the soul that receives it a capacity for the grace of the priesthood, nor has that grace power to engender it; but, on the contrary, the holy unction supposes it and necessitates it, as it is in itself a plenitude for the fulfilment of that capacity and for the bestowal of other gifts, in order that the soul of the priest may receive with ever new fulness, not Christ, because it possesses Him entirely, but His divine spirit, His adorable virtues, His quickening grace, His unspeakable light, His infinite merits.

By strengthening and hallowing the aptitudes bestowed upon the soul by creating and redeeming grace, the sacerdotal unction gives them a marvellous development, leading to other more sublime and divine aptitudes.

The soul of the priest, thus consecrated, adorned, and embellished, is in all truth the dwelling-place which Incarnate Wisdom has built for herself, in which she has hewn out seven pillars and set forth a table whereat souls are to be fed.

The light shows to me that the seven pillars of this living temple represent the seven gifts of the Holy Ghost, which the soul of the priest receives in all their fulness by the imposition of hands—a grace which communicates to the priest the power of begetting Jesus in souls and forming them to the spirit and to the grace of God our Saviour.

In this living abode the Divine Wisdom has spread another table, wherefrom souls are to be nourished and strengthened. This divine table is the treasure of holy writ, wherein are contained the light and the grace which are the life of souls.

By giving His divine spirit to the soul of

the priest, Jésus gives him thereby the key of the sacred treasury. Henceforth the priest is obliged by mission and by office to break the bread of the divine Word for souls, so as to nourish them with the hidden substance it contains.

February 12, 1880. I said yesterday that the soul of the priest is shown to me as a most pure mirror, in which God reflects almost substantially His adorable perfections.

The light of grace reveals to me that every soul bears the reflection of some of the divine perfections, and that the sanctity of each flows from the particular manner in which it has to reflect God's divine attributes.

It is, however, shown to me that there is no creature capable of bearing directly the effects of the divine perfections; that they can receive only the divine effusions of them, be subject to their operations, and receive the manifestation of them made by God outside Himself, which manifestation is received by them in the way of reflection.

The Sacred Manhood of Jesus alone amongst all creatures, forming, through the hypostatic union, one only person with the Divine Word, has been made capable of bearing directly the effects of the adorable perfections of the Godhead.

It alone can endure the infinite sanctity of God, who finds stains in all created purity; it alone can exist in presence of the Divine Omnipotence, one direct act of which would reduce the whole of creation to nothingness.

It alone can endure the blows of Divine Justice, one stroke of which would crush all creatures, from which the Sacred Manhood has suffered so terribly that it has been slain by them, and entirely, as it were, reduced to naught.

The soul of the priest cannot bear directly the effects of the divine attributes. However, by a singular privilege, communicated to it by the sacred character of the priesthood, the consecrated soul reflects the divine perfections and receives their adorable effusions in a special way.

Furthermore, it bears them directly, not indeed by itself, but by Christ, to whom it is united by a very special bond.

The priest is not only the subject of the operations of the divine perfections, but he is the instrument of these operations. Christ invests him substantially in Himself with His own divine power, and places in his hands, in virtue of this supreme power, the rights of His infinite justice and mercy. His patience, His long-suffering, His compassionate goodness, His charity for souls, have in some sort become incarnate in him. In sum, he is the limit which God has imposed on His own sovereign independence.

My words cannot express all that my soul conceives concerning these great mysteries of infinite power and love.

The interior light emits flashes and rays that nothing can reflect; and by this divine light the priesthood appears to me something so great, so divine, that the eyes of my soul could not without a special grace sustain such a vision.

In its behalf I see that God has in a way exhausted all the treasures of His divine riches; that He has made it the created manifestation of Himself; a living shrine, from which are reflected, as from so many precious stones, all that which can be revealed of His adorable perfections outside Himself; that His immense and infinite love has completed the divine richness and beauty of this living shrine, by setting in its midst His substantial and living image, His Incarnate Word.

This divine state of the priesthood has been established by God upon three foundations or elements, which, blended in a wonderful unity, give it its true form. These three elements are shown to me to be the Divine Power or authority, knowledge, and holiness.

It is shown to me that in the divine institution of the priesthood it was the will of Jesus that these three constituents should be inseparable.

July 28, 1880. During the rest that Jesus in the Host deigned to give me last night, my soul received a lively impression of the evil that is done to souls by the captivity of truth.

The interior light showed to me that souls are weakened, lose day by day their spiritual strength, languish and die away in ever-increasing torpor and sloth ; and of this class, which comprises the greater number of souls, many there are who have only the semblance of life, having lost its energy and powers.

This same light revealed to me that one of the great causes of this universal evil is this, that souls are no longer fed with the truth in its purity, in its simplicity, in its vivifying and regenerating power ; that the bread which is broken to them has lost its savour, its power of nourishment, which alone can support and develop spiritual life, and all to give it a flavour that pleases souls, but leaves them in their weakness, without strength, without courage, for the austere practice of the fundamental virtues of Christianity.

I do not know whether it is the light of Jesus which discovers these things to me, or whether they are the effect of an illusion ; it is nevertheless true that they make a deep impression on my heart, which feels some little of the bitterness of the suffering which I see they cause to the sacred Heart and divine Soul of Jesus in the Host.

It was shown to me that another great defect in some consecrated ministers, dispensers of the bread of the Word of Life, is that they stop at the surface of the sacred truths of the Word of God, without penetrating into the substance of these truths; that they do not enter into the deep and hidden sense of the Sacred Word, to draw therefrom the essence of life which it contains; that they give as food to souls only the outward form of the truth, and not the truth itself.

Because the unction of the grace of God does not accompany their words, it follows that souls take a dislike to both the rind and the fruit itself; and that, rejecting the truth, they seek their food in vanities and lies, looking to satisfy their craving hunger and burning thirst with that which can only increase their hunger and their thirst.

Would that I could express, as it is given to me to see it, what Jesus suffers, in His mystical members, from the neglect of these ministers, these consecrated dispensers! How keen, how devouring the hunger and the thirst of our dear Saviour to deliver from their captivity His own love, His holy truth, in order that souls might be rescued from the shameful bonds of sin, and all that which fetters and hinders them from advancing in the way of perfection might be swept away; that a complete manifestation might be made of the greatest excess of His love!

I saw the Sacred Heart of Jesus in the Host burning with the most ardent desire to make the truth known to souls, because truth assures the cure of weakness, the revival of liberty and peace; love triumphs, life springs up, the work of transformation and deification begins: because the truth is Jesus Himself; it is our loving Saviour appearing to the soul in His mercy, revealing Himself by the effects of His divine and tender charity, attracting the soul with strength and sweetness to serve Him, to love Him, to glorify Him.

But to make known the truth which thus delivers souls from captivity and imparts to them so many blessings, Jesus in the Host stands in need of labourers who will unreservedly devote themselves to this divine work; and because this work is a holy one, it is the will of our Divine Master that the labourer should also be holy, to do his work well, in order that nature may not debase any of the acts of his ministry.

The consecrated minister, therefore, ought to enter upon His divine work with a true evangelical spirit, so as not to bring into it the spirit of the world; with the devoted and disinterested zeal of an apostle, to allow no human interest ever to profane it.

In a word, he ought to work, not as a mercenary, but as a true son of our Heavenly Father, in the sight of whom he is another Jesus; as a worthy lieutenant of Christ, as His successor in His divine work; as a faithful organ of the Holy Ghost, not forgetful, however, that all these titles of greatness do not exclude a state of servitude which the Divine Master Himself has undergone. For in His priests and by His priests Jesus wishes to continue to be what He was upon earth, and what He is still under the Eucharistic veils, viz., the servant of God, His Father; the servant of men, His brethren; a public, universal servant.

As Jesus has justified this name of servant by all sorts of labours and sacrifices; as He justifies it now by so many self-sacrifices, by humiliation, annihilation of self, and obedience, it is the will of our Divine Saviour that they in their turn, who have the privilege of sharing His office, should also bear the name in the same way; that is, that they should justify it by their works, at the expense of their strength, of their time, by the sacrifice of their pleasures and of their personal interests, by giving up all, even themselves; and as He Himself has devoted His sacred soul and sacrificed His life for souls, so also those whom He associates in His divine ministry should every day devote and sacrifice their life and all that they are for the souls they have begotten to the life of Christ, and for those they have to bring to birth in the future.

It is shown to me that in the divine work of His revelation, of His manifestation, Jesus could well afford to act without the aid of His creature, by Himself to reveal His truth to souls and establish there the reign of His love. But what He could do He has not done, will not do, and even makes it impossible for Himself to do. It is the will of our loving Saviour, in the counsels of His infinite wisdom, of His immense and incomprehensible love for souls, to make use of man. He deigns to employ him, and puts Himself in the necessity of standing in some way in need of him to do His divine work and extend His kingdom.

It is certain that from the Eucharist, where He personally abides, our most sweet Jesus sends forth over His Church, as a body, and upon each of her members, the rays of His divine grace, His love, His truth, His light. He has concentrated them substantially in His Sacred Manhood, as in a divine centre, that they may thence be unceasingly poured forth over the multitudes, which form part of His mystical body, not only the living members of that body, but also those that are dead to the life of the soul, that they may be raised up again.

But as there are multitudes of souls who never approach this fount of love, who scarcely ever turn themselves towards this divine centre of Truth and of Light, to be enlightened by its quickening rays, Jesus, wishing not a single soul to be deprived of these divine influences, has made of the priesthood a secondary centre, in order directly and visibly to shed on every soul the influences of His light, of His truth, of His love. Thus one of the greatest obligations, one of the most binding duties of the priest is to live in such manner that his soul may always be a luminous centre, a burning light; Jesus having chosen him to be the light of the world. It is the will of Jesus that all His priests should be burning and shining lights in His holy Church—burning by sanctity, shining by knowledge.

As a light in order to be a true light, to enlighten all around, should unite the two conditions—of being consumed in burning and of giving light in being consumed—and as one of these conditions without the other would render the light useless, so it is not sufficient that the soul of the priest should burn with the fire of zeal and be consumed in the works it inspires; it must also be full of light so as to shine, that is to say, that it should be endowed with knowledge and labour constantly to increase its treasure.

I cannot say what the interior light reveals to me of the sorrow felt by the Sacred Heart of Jesus in the Host, when He sees His ministers sunder what He has so admirably united in the priesthood.

July 30, 1880. Jesus has reassured me, tormented by an inward fear when I prayed for the renewal of the spirit and grace of the priesthood in the ministers of the altar. Fearful that I was so losing time that I should have employed in meditating on Jesus in the Host, in the mysteries of His Eucharistic life, I asked my most dear Master to deliver me from this preoccupation of mind, so that I might have full and entire liberty to think of Him alone, of Him in His life on the altar, in His life of union with souls.

I had not as yet expressed this desire, this need of my soul, when Jesus deigned to say to me: " Am I not free to make use of thee according to My good pleasure ? Is it not just that thou shouldst wish and desire nothing but what I wish and desire Myself? Give thyself up without reserve and without objection to the work that My grace gives thee to do, and do not imagine that thou honourest Me more by thinking of Me in the Eucharist than by thinking of Me in the priesthood; for My life in the sacrament of love, and My life in the priesthood, are both one and the same life. Hidden, annihilated, powerless in the one, I am revealed, rendered visible, invested with My own power in the other; and the mysteries which are contained in these two forms of the same life—these two modes of the same presence—are equally unknown, despised."

I heard these words this morning, whilst I was in adoration before Jesus in the Host. This evening, as I was meditating upon Him, my Divine Saviour deigned to repeat them again, with additions: " My desire, My will about thee is that thou shouldst employ thyself only and entirely in honouring, glorifying, loving, and making others love My presence, My life in the Eucharist; My presence, My life in the priesthood—both mysteries, in the same degree ignored, in which I am alike despised and set at naught ".

For some length of time, of which I could give no account, my soul remained entirely overwhelmed by these words and by the light which showed me that in order to fulfil the desire, the designs of Jesus upon me, I had nothing else to do but to give myself up freely, and at every instant, to His divine operations, without ever so much as looking to past or future action, simply absorbed in that of the present moment, without any thought as to the means that I should make use of, but using them just as Jesus would put them in my hands.

My soul was terrified at the sight and feeling of this death to all action, to al personal work, and yet it earnestly desired it, and offered itself to it with all the strength of its will; because it saw in it the founda tion, the cause, the necessary principle of the life and action of Jesus in us.

July 31, 1880. As I was in the choir,

Jesus in the Host deigned to draw me powerfully to Himself, and to unite my soul to Him by the perception of His life and of His presence in the priesthood.

Having drawn me all to Himself, this most sweet Master led me first to contemplate the deep sorrow of His Sacred Heart, the bitter sufferings of His most holy soul, arising always from the same causes. I was then strongly pressed to give myself to the work of reparation, at the request of Jesus, who deigned to say to me: "Come, make Me amends for these insults; console Me in the sorrow caused by the indifference the hearts of some priests show for My dearest interests; the little love and respect with which they treat me; the want of reverence which they have for My Sacred Person". The interior light then showed me because Jesus in the Host has, by an excess of incomprehensible love, rendered Himself dependent, not on the merit and personal sanctity of His ministers, but on the power conferred upon them by Him, on their will, on their intention in the exercise of that power; this dependence is to

Him a constant humiliation, the cause of His greatest sorrows, of the most bitter of the pains of His Sacred Heart.

What my soul saw, what it felt, I could not express; I only experienced a cruel anguish, the strength of which overpowered me, to see that in many consecrated souls the priestly spirit had lost, and was losing every day, some of its vitality; that the grace of the priesthood was weakened in the same degree, that it was losing its purity, its power, and vivifying influence over souls.

I heard at the same time an interior voice say to me: "If a soul could comprehend what outrages Jesus suffers, what contempt on the part of those souls who do not live as they ought, according to the spirit of their divine vocation; what His sacred soul has to endure in being unable, for this very reason, to reveal Himself as much as required by His love; if that soul could comprehend this two-fold suffering of Jesus in the Host, howsoever little was the love that it had for this Divine Saviour, yet there is no sacrifice it would not feel bound to impose upon itself, to obtain from God holy priests for His Church, worthy ministers of Jesus in the Host, faithful and zealous preachers of the mysteries of His Eucharistic life".

At the same time that I heard these words in the depths of my soul, a bright light showed me that the revelation, the manifestation, the knowledge of Jesus, are in a certain way bound up with the holiness of life of the priest, that, in a certain way and in a certain measure, they depend on it; that the life of the priest ought to be the visible revelation, the development of that of Jesus, the irradiation of His light; that all his works ought to give out the sweet odour of the virtues of Christ, and his actions to shed a living balm, to distil upon souls the quickening fragrance of His life. This same light discovered to me new depths in the sorrows which flood His Eucharistic Heart, when He sees the souls, which His love had made to be lights and sources of light, become dark as night to those for whom they ought to be like day.

I saw how necessary, how indispensable it is that, in order to spread light always and on every side, the life of the priest should be hidden and buried in the life of Christ, so that the latter only should be seen in him; for, though hidden, the life of the priest is, and must necessarily be, open to all, his least actions exercising an almost incalculable influence on the minds and hearts of all around him.

In virtue of the grace of priesthood, even when he does not make actual use of it, by the very fact of his presence, the priest who lives according to the spirit of his divine vocation exercises a real and most powerful action over the world of souls.

While meditating on these things which grace had revealed to me, I was led to pray still more earnestly for the renewal of the spirit of the priesthood, for the glory of Jesus in the Host, and the salvation of souls.

March 1, 1881. Adoration of the Forty Hours. To fulfil a duty, from which it was not thought proper to dispense me, I have just left the presence of Jesus in the Host quite heart-broken. I hoped that the sacrifice I had made in leaving the choir would have obtained for me the grace to overcome the repugnance I have to writing; but Jesus will not have it so, He leaves me entirely to my helplessness, which is crushing me more and more.

Three times have I tried to take up my pen, and for nearly half-an-hour I have been struggling against this invincible weakness, which causes me unusual suffering, which I do not understand.

The visions which Jesus deigned to show me during these two days of Exposition, the impressions that they have produced on my soul, are still seen and felt by me; and yet, fettered by the bonds of this terrible weakness, I find it impossible to relate them, I cannot find a single word to explain them.

All that I can say is that the sublime and divine dignity of the priesthood is almost always before the eyes of my soul; and that my constant occupation is to make amends to Jesus in the Host for the outrages, the contempt, the wounds inflicted on His Heart in the Holy Eucharist by those priests who do not live up to the standard of their divine vocation, who do not render the honour and respect they ought to their sublime dignity.

The thoughts and visions of my soul are a true mystery to me, especially at the present moment, for during these days of Exposition it should have been my duty to pray to Jesus, to comfort His Heart in the Holy Eucharist by making reparation for the outrages and the indifference of souls. I ought to have meditated on His Eucharistic mysteries, and, behold! all these works have been impossible for me, my soul being all the while taken captive and all-absorbed by meditations on the priesthood. During these three days Jesus only revealed Himself in this way to me; in no other way did He draw and unite my soul to Him; moreover, I do not know what I did during the time spent in the presence of my dear Lord; my soul is lost, I know not where I am. . . .

The fear that I had lost my time, and with it all the graces that Jesus would have granted me during those days of benediction—the fear that the thoughts and visions which had been before my soul were only illusions—

caused me indescribable suffering, which rendered me quite incapable of giving an account of all I had seen and felt.

March 6, 1881. The insight that Jesus grants me into the greatness, sublime dignity, and divine power of the priesthood is still continued, and, as it becomes deeper and more profound, passes understanding. It is to me an infinite abyss wherein my soul is lost, wherein it rests on happiness inexpressible, though, at the same time, it experiences an equal amount of suffering.

While filling me with peace, with happiness, with something unspeakable, which overspreads my soul with an effusion of grace, the nature of which I cannot explain—while leaving me in a profound calm, these visions of the priesthood are a cause of pain, of interior suffering, to me, because they reveal to me the great sorrows of the Heart of Jesus in the Host, and leave me with an undefinable impression which is the chief cause of the anguish which crushes and overwhelms my soul.

These visions bring me also an ever-recurring fear of being deceived, of losing time. Hence I make incessant but useless efforts to escape from this state of mind ; but the thoughts and feelings caused by them weigh more heavily upon my soul and carry it captive the more I struggle against them. Their action, their influence, are exerted incessantly upon all my faculties, keep them fettered ; and, when not engaged in duty or exterior work, they absorb me completely.

I am confounded, overwhelmed, that Jesus in the Host deigns to give me understanding and makes me feel so powerfully His life, His presence, His work, His indwelling in the priesthood.

To obey Jesus, who strongly draws me, I will endeavour, in spite of all my weakness, to give an account of the visions He vouchsafes me.

The first vision of the priesthood that Jesus gave me a few days ago is continually before the eyes of my soul. It represents to me generally, but in a very distinct and luminous manner, the sublime dignity, the divine power of the priesthood, and shows me that, being essentially bound up with the Eucharist, it is in union with it the life, the light, the strength, the stay of souls; that it enlightens, purifies, and sanctifies them by dispensing to them the mysteries of God, the infinite treasures of the merits of Christ, the riches of grace, the Author Himself of grace.

This same vision shows to me that although only the souls invested with the sacred character possess the divine dignity and power of the priesthood, yet that all souls partake of its divine influences and live by its operation. I see that the priesthood is not only an active power in the Church, but is of itself a living and quickening power, possessing in itself a real source of grace, a principle of life, to be given and communicated to souls; and that because the priesthood is not only the most complete representation of Jesus, His most perfect image, but because it is Jesus Himself continuing the office of His supreme and divine mission, either towards God His Father, or in behalf of souls.

To Jesus living in His holy Church I see the priesthood is the supplement of His existence. My dear Saviour shows Himself to the eyes of my soul as really present, living and working in the priesthood as He is living and working in the Eucharist; and, while allowing me to dwell upon Himself, upon His Heart, in the holy Eucharist, in the life, the action, the work which He accomplishes in these two unspeakable gifts conferred upon the world by His love, Jesus shows me how few are the souls who remember to give Him thanks for the blessing of the priesthood. How hurtful to His Sacred Heart is this unthankfulness for the greatest of His gifts and ingratitude in living and feeding upon the blessings of which this gift is the fruitful source, without thinking of Him or making Him any return!

In revealing to me that the want of gratitude for the blessing of the priesthood is a cause of sorrow to His Heart, Jesus shows me that no affliction can equal that which He feels when priestly souls, forgetting the sublime dignity of their sacred character, do not live the exalted life to which they have been called; do not pay the honour and respect they owe to His constant presence and indwelling within them; do not imitate His life; and do not wholly and entirely depend on His divine operation and work in them and by them.

It is absolutely impossible for me to express in words what the interior light reveals to me in all these things; much more still to recount the deep sorrows of the Heart of Jesus in the Host such as He shows them to me, and enables me to enter into them.

When I try to turn myself away from them, I seem to hear within my soul these words, which fix my mind on thoughts from which I would fain be free: "My daughter, why wouldst thou cease to console Me in the most bitter of My Eucharistic sorrows? In what more noble work couldst thou employ thy life? Occupy thyself with Me according to My good pleasure; give thyself up to Me without a word.

March 10, 1881. Last night, in the silence of weakness, while intent on the contemplation of Jesus in His Eucharistic state, and uniting myself therein to the workings of His sacred soul, I felt myself attracted by a vision, which revealed to me what Jesus is in the priest and the priest in Jesus.

Though these things seem to me, and are, in fact, impossible to describe as they really are, I feel that I must make an effort to give an account of them as far as I shall be able. The interior light first made me understand that what Jesus is to God, and the Sacred Manhood to the Incarnate Word, that the priest is to Jesus.

As Jesus is the substantial image of the invisible God, and receives of the Father in His eternal birth the Godhead, with all its infinite perfections, and in His temporal birth the grace of the personal union of the Word with His Sacred Manhood; so, likewise, the priest, being the visible image of Jesus, receives from Him His mission, His power, His dignity, His whole grace.

Again, as Jesus is anointed, consecrated, sanctified by the grace of the hypostatic union, so the priest, by the unction of the priesthood, which is a participation of the unction bestowed by the Godhead on the Sacred Manhood, is made a Christ, anointed by Jesus Himself, and consecrated above all other Christs.

In the same manner as the Sacred Manhood belongs entirely to God, in an unspeakable way, being united with the Godhead by the substantial bond of the personality of the Word—union by which it lives, subsists, and operates in the Word and by the Word, though by its creation it is infinitely below the Word; in like manner, the priest, by the sacerdotal consecration, receives a grace which sanctifies and consecrates to God for eternity the substance, the essence itself of his soul, and dedicates his whole person to Him, by uniting it immediately to the first Christ, to Jesus, the beginning of all grace and sanctification; uniting it in such a way as to have no other subsistence in his mind and will, no other way of working but in Jesus and by the power of His spirit; so that all his acts are in Him, of Him, and for Him. Since God the Father does everything in nature by His word, since the Word does everything in grace by His Manhood, as by an instrument united to Him, in unity of person, so Jesus, Man-God, acts and pours out His graces on souls by the priest, as by an instrument united to Him in unity of spirit and of grace, to work their sanctification.

March 11, 1881. Yesterday my dear Jesus revealed Himself to me in the priest, and showed me the priest in Himself.

After considering for a long time in this vision that the priest is to Jesus what Jesus is to God, the interior light which filled my soul showed me that the priest is to Jesus in the Eucharist what the Sacred Manhood is to the Divine Word.

I saw then, or rather I understood, that as the Sacred Manhood, united with the Godhead in hypostatic unity by the Person of the Word, is made in and by this Divine Word the organ and universal cause of all supernatural operations; that as it serves as an instrument to the Eternal Word in the execution of all the works of His mercy and of His love; so likewise the priest, depending upon Christ, being under the influence of His spirit and of His grace, in participation and communication with His divine power and authority, is to Jesus a subordinate instrument which, most intimately bound and united to Him by the character of the priesthood, serves Him in the execution of His own operations, in the continuation and completion of these same works of mercy and of love.

Again, as God operates and does all things outside Himself, by His Word, as the Word executes the divine decrees and does all things by His Sacred Manhood, in like manner also this Word made Man, living and working invisibly in His holy Church, does and works everything visibly by the priest, whom He has made another self by the sacred character, which has impressed upon him His living likeness, and has established him as a mediator between souls and Himself, as He Himself is in a higher and more perfect way our Mediator before God the Father.

For this and all other offices of His sublime and divine mission, Jesus has invested the priest with the sovereign power and authority which in His Sacred Manhood He has received from God the Father,—an authority which gives to the priest right and power over the whole order of grace, to bring it to pass and confer it by his sacred ministry, being constituted by office a channel for the outpourings of the grace and of the love of Jesus.

This authority extends not only over the order of grace, but over the Author Himself of grace, for the priest has power and authority over Jesus Himself, to bring Him present on the altar, to give Him to souls, and to offer Him to God.

This authority also gives him power over souls to sanctify them, to beget them to God, to form Jesus in them; for the consecration of the priesthood gives to the priest a grace which tends to produce Jesus, His spirit, His life in souls—a grace which is like the fulness which was given to Mary to conceive by the Holy Ghost and bring forth Jesus. This grace was shown to me as a living, inexhaustible, ever-springing fount which Jesus would fain see perpetually flowing over souls—the flow of which, when checked and kept captive, causes His sacred soul one of its greatest afflictions.

Still in the same light and through it, I saw that the priestly vocation has a twofold mission, which forms its essence, which is the end of its existence to which all the life and labours of the priest ought to be referred—the service, the glory, the honour of Jesus in the Eucharist—the sanctification of souls for the same glory. This divine mission binds the priest to a loving relationship, intimacy with Jesus, a constant and entire dependence on Him, to render to Him the honour, glory, and homage, which by state of life and by duty he ought to render to Him in the sacrament of His love, because the priesthood has been established only for the Eucharist and on account of the Eucharist; and the life, the mind, the glory of the priest belong entirely to Jesus in the Host to honour Him by continuing His divine priesthood, to reveal the ineffable and divine life of the Word in the Sacred Manhood, and the life of this Sacred Manhood in the Divine Word; for the priest ought to bear in himself an image of this life of Jesus, and share in His grace and holiness as he bears the character of the priesthood and partakes of its power; consequently, the priest's life, the habits, the actions of his life, do not belong to himself but to Jesus, to whom he is consecrated and dedicated as His minister.

April 7, 1881. I would fain tell what I saw of the beauty of the living altar of Jesus —the soul of the priest. This beauty is something unspeakable, beyond words to say. I saw it arose from the three following causes: viz., the consecration of that living altar, its sanctification, and its possession.

The consecration is made not only of the soul and of its inmost substance, as the noblest and worthiest part of the altar, but also of the substance of the body which receives its exterior mark and bears its impress.

I saw that this consecration is effected not only by the gifts of a very special grace by the impress of a sacred and external character, but by the Sacred Manhood of Jesus, who is upon this living altar not for a time only, not only while His sacrifice lasts, but is united to it in a permanent manner, dwelling there and abiding there by a sort of personal presence, which makes the priest a kind of fulness of His sacred Person.

I saw that this personal presence of Jesus in the priest, His permanent indwelling in him, His abiding in him by title of a particular and special possession, is like the high and unspeakable way in which the Divine Word dwells in the Sacred Manhood, and is not a simple figure, but a living image of it full of reality.

By virtue of the sacerdotal unction, which is a participation of the unction given by the Godhead to the Sacred Manhood, the priest is anointed and consecrated to receive a particular communication of created graces, which flow from the divine consecration of the Sacred Manhood. He enters into privileges reserved to himself alone, and becomes by dependence on Jesus, by participation of His divine rights, what our Divine Saviour is Himself by essence.

It is impossible for me to express in words what my soul saw, what it understood, when Jesus set before my mind this great mystery of love and of divine power in Himself and in the priest. I saw the beginning, the cause of it, in Jesus, and in the priest its accomplishment, its living reality.

There were not two distinct visions, bearing upon separate objects, but one vision of one subject only; for I saw Jesus so intimately bound up with the priest, and the priest so entirely lost, so completely effaced in this Lamb of God that was slain, that the eyes of my soul could perceive one only and divine whole, in which I continued to see, without being able to explain how, the Lamb of God and His living altar, distinct, yet in a special way united.

Lost in an ocean of light which dazzled my sight without taking away from it the power of seeing, my soul then contemplated the other mystery. It saw that, as the Sacred Manhood of Jesus is the altar of the living God, on which the Eternal Word, in adoration of the Divine Majesty, and for the salvation, unceasingly offers, by that altar, and by that deified soul, which is united with Him, the sacrifices of praise, of thanksgiving, of prayer, of reparation, that are most pleasing to God the Father, and most worthy of His

Sovereign Majesty, in whom, and by whom, all other sacrifices are received and accepted. In like manner the priest is made the living temple of Jesus in the Host, and his soul the most precious altar of His adorable Manhood, an animated altar, on which, and by which, the Lamb of God sacrifices Himself in continuation of His office of Universal Adorer and Saviour.

On this living altar of atonement Jesus, Man-God, the only propitiation for the sins of the world, unceasingly offers to God His Father, by His sacred soul, the sacrifice of perpetual adoration, of continual praise, of universal supplication and infinite reparation, for on that altar Jesus sacrifices Himself for all souls.

Jesus has given me to understand that His life, His presence, His indwelling in the priest, is for the general good of souls; that He inhabits this living temple, and is there in unceasing action and work for the entire Church.

April 12, 1881. As on Sunday, during my thanksgiving, Jesus showed me what

His sacrifice is in the soul of the priest, how the communion of the priest differs from that of the faithful—not as to the participation of His sacred body, but in the effects—the fruits which it should produce in the world of souls. During that meditation it seemed to me that my dear Saviour addressed me in these words, still appearing to me identified with His living altar: " Behold, here is My true altar of propitiation, the living tabernacle of God among men, which I consecrate and sanctify by Myself to be a sanctuary filled by the Most High, not only in His immensity, as in the rest of creation, but by a fulness and most intimate presence of His Godhead, by communications and special bestowal of His adorable perfections".

I then saw that there is in the soul of the priest a threefold fulness, rendering it a worthy dwelling-place of the Most High; a fulness of grace which is a participation of that chief fulness of grace which is in the Sacred Manhood of Jesus; a fulness not only of the gifts, of the accidental graces of the Holy Ghost, but of the substance itself of these gifts, of this grace, and of the Person Itself of the Divine Spirit; a fulness of Jesus, Man-God, who is the Author of grace in His Sacred Manhood and the cause of the Holy Ghost in the adorable Trinity.

These three excellent gifts of fulness dedicate the soul of the priest to God made Man to serve as a living altar for the sacrifice of His sacred body, of His precious blood; and because of this sacrifice the Holy Trinity makes of it a special abode to receive the praise, the glory rendered to It by the sacrifice of the Lamb of God.

This vision ended in showing me that these three kinds of fulness ought to be perpetually flowing upon souls, for the priest does not receive them for himself alone.

April 13, 1881. After Holy Communion, at the moment in which I renewed the entire surrender of myself to Jesus in the Host, this Lamb of God offered in sacrifice drew me entirely to Himself, and showing me His Heart in the Eucharist, it seemed to me that He addressed me thus:

" During these days I wish thy only occupation to be to contemplate the infinite love of My Heart for men, that thou shouldst give Me thanks for the two great means by which I have made it an ever-operating gift ".

I then saw in a brilliant light these two means, viz., the Eucharist and the priesthood; and my soul entered on the contemplation of the latter in a manner that I cannot explain. All its powers were seized, absorbed by the vision of the sublimity of the priesthood, and all occupied in thanking Jesus for having made this divine gift to men, for having given such power and might to the priest.

I saw that the Eucharist and the priesthood are united so closely by ties and bonds so unspeakable as to make in a certain way one and the same gift of the love of the Heart of the Man-God; that they are two modes of one and the same presence of Jesus Christ in His Church,—two forms of His life therein.

The grace of the priesthood was shown to me as high above all other graces, forming an order quite apart and separate. I saw that it drew its pre-eminence from two causes: from the cause from which it comes—the fulness of the grace which is in the Sacred Manhood of Jesus, and from the end or effect for which it is given.

It seemed to me to be in the Church as a river of life, a living, an ever-flowing source of all the graces which nourish, fertilise, and sanctify souls: not that it is a cause in itself, but because it makes of him who receives it an instrument of the effects of grace, and a channel of its flowing.

While showing me these things, Jesus said to me: " How few are the souls who remember to thank Me for the gift of the priesthood. I wish thee to take upon thyself this tribute of gratitude, which is so neglected. . . . It is not from thyself that thou shouldst draw the gratitude that I ask of thee, but from Me, who am the living and substantial thanksgiving. I wish thee to make this thanksgiving by Myself; and, to that effect, unceasingly to offer to the Holy Trinity, as a homage for the blessing of the priesthood, the divine cause from which it comes, the living fount from which it perpetually springs: that is to say, My Heart in the Eucharist, My sacred Soul, which at this moment are substantially united to thee, which I give to thee in order to make of them a perpetual oblation to God My Father; in order to make this offering of My adorable Person thine own, thou hast only to penetrate into the secret of My interior life and enter into My Heart, to unite thyself to the working of My sacred Soul and give thyself up in the silence of complete abandonment to My divine operations. By so doing, thou shalt console Me in one of My most bitter sorrows—that of the ingratitude of men, of their want of acknowledgment for the most excellent of My gifts."

April 20, 1881. During a great part of the day, on Maundy Thursday, Jesus fixed my thoughts in contemplation in Himself of the greatness of the priesthood, which He has instituted to continue and perpetuate the functions of His divine and eternal priesthood, of which it is in this way a substantial participation. In this meditation I saw above all the power, the efficacious and truly divine virtue, of the grace of the priesthood. I saw that grace born in God with Jesus; and, at the same moment as that one and only Sovereign Priest of the Most High, I saw it abiding in its fulness in the Sacred Manhood of the Eternal Word, made sacrificing priest and victim of God the Father.

I saw the source and cause of that grace in the Divine Word, who, by the hypostatic union, as by a personal unction united to the first anointing made by the Godhead, consecrated the Sacred Manhood to be the Sovereign and Eternal Priest of God, in whom ought to be anointed and consecrated all other priests, who are made Christs by participation of this first consecration and unction of Jesus.

I saw that this grace had resided in the Sacred Manhood only until the day of the institution of the priesthood, and that then was made the first outpouring of this divine grace which the Apostles were the first to receive.

I wish I could describe the manner in which this divine outpouring was shown me;

but it is not possible for me. There is nothing so beautiful, so great, so unspeakable, as that vision in which I saw the Sacred Heart of Jesus as an infinite abyss, as an unfathomable and boundless ocean of love for God His Father, and for men, the redemption of whom He was about to accomplish.

From this abyss, from this divine ocean, I saw the grace of the priesthood issuing like an impetuous torrent of life and love; and this torrent I saw showering its divine waters upon all the Church of God, overflowing, quickening, regenerating, and sanctifying all.

By it there was in Jesus a complete, living, and ever-actual overflow of the power given Him by the Father of His divine authority; in one word, of that which is greatest in Him — His eternal priesthood.

By that overflow of His whole self in His holy Church, Jesus gives solace to the twofold love, which as a devouring fire unceasingly consumes His adorable Heart.

Jesus, wishing to honour and glorify the Father to the end by the sacrifice of His Sacred Manhood, the only worthy offering to the majesty of His Father, and being no longer in a state to continue this sacrifice by sufferings and death, devised by a miracle of His omnipotence the marvellous plan of the priesthood. In order to continue to perpetuate the holocaust of His sacred Person by the ministry of priests, and to offer up day by day to God His Father, by and in their hands, His own body as upon living altars, He established the priesthood, founded upon a real participation of the most divine of His functions, making of those who were to exercise it a living continuation of His Sacred Manhood.

This is why the priest offers up the sacrifice not only in the name of Jesus, by His divine authority, but also in His sacred Person; for it is Jesus Himself who offers the sacrifice by the ministry of His priests.

Thus the priest is used as an instrument by Jesus to place Himself, in His glorious and impassible flesh, in a state of true and perpetual holocaust, to be always present before the throne of the Father in the appearance of Host and Victim really slain, entirely and constantly offered to His honour and to His glory, in the name and for the love of the poor creatures whom He has redeemed and washed in His divine blood, whom He redeems anew and more abundantly at every Eucharistic shedding of His precious blood.

This it was given me to contemplate in the very Heart of Jesus Himself in the Host; and to see it not in figures and images, but in its truth, living and working in its divine reality.

I saw again in this Eucharistic Heart, that as it is to God alone that sacrifice may be offered, and as it belongs to Jesus alone to offer it, as having an infinite dignity, equal to the Sovereign Majesty whom the sacrifice is meant to honour and to glorify, it also belongs to Jesus, Man-God, alone to establish the priesthood of the law of grace, to have, to make, to consecrate, priests, to be for Him living instruments for the continuation of His sovereign priesthood.

In showing me these mysteries of love and of divine power, Jesus seemed to say to me:

"My daughter, from the first instant that

the grace of the priesthood issued forth from My Heart as from a divine fountain, it has never ceased, and shall never cease to flow from it with the same fulness, the same power, the same virtue, the same purity: with a living, everflowing stream ".

I understood then that this grace is annexed not to the person of the sacred minister, but to the priesthood itself; and that being independent of personal dispositions, it is always given with the sacred character, as being the inheritance of the priesthood, and being a part of its essence for the use and the sacred functions which directly belong to it; so that by this grace, which is the power, the virtue itself, of Christ Jesus, all that the priest does in virtue and by the power of his holy ministry remains holy, whatever his disposition and personal holiness.

I understood, also, that, besides these great effects of the grace and power of the priesthood, the grace of the priesthood is given to the priest as a source of many influences of life and of holiness, which, to be produced in souls, require personal holiness in the minister, and are on that account dependent on his dispositions. This grace is given also as a living and active power, the exercise of which demands the special co-operation of the priest, as well as his personal devotedness, so that in proportion as holiness falls short and zeal is lacking, in the same measure the grace of the priesthood is held captive and without fruit in the soul itself of the priest, and through it in the souls over whom this grace ought to exercise its influence, to produce in them the life of Jesus—holiness.

April 24, 1881. These three last days during all the time of my thanksgiving, though I had a deep sentiment of my union with Jesus, yet I could only contemplate this Lamb of God offered in sacrifice, present and living in the sacred minister in virtue of a peculiar identification of an order apart; and I saw the priest so closely bound up, so intimately and indissolubly united to Jesus in the Host, that he was completely absorbed and totally effaced in Him. There remained Jesus alone, showing Himself to me in the priest as through a transparent veil, so luminous and so clearly seen that the veil itself seemed to disappear.

I would fain render an account of the vision that was given me of this deification; but the things that have been revealed to me are so great, so high, so unspeakable, that they pass understanding and the power of words to express them.

All I can say is that Jesus and the priest are not only united but are one without confusion, because in that inexpressible identification and union Jesus and the priest are distinct but not divided. There is a mutual life of Jesus in the priest and of the priest in Jesus; and this is the life which makes the perfect harmony and the true essence of this admirable unity, wherein the priest appears to me only as a living homage to the divinely human life of the Eternal Word in the Sacred Manhood, and to the humanly divine life of this adorable Manhood in the Word of Life, in whom It subsists.

The presence and the life of Jesus in the priest are shown to me to be at the same time a living image of the mutual life of the Three

Divine Persons one in the other, and also a kind of extension, a true continuation of the double form of the essentially one life of the Word in the Sacred Manhood and of the Sacred Manhood in the Divine Word, in virtue of which the priest is by participation what Jesus is Himself by essence and by fulness —the eldest Son amongst all creatures of the Holy Trinity, the Christ, the Anointed of God.

But, again, how can I express in words these high and sublime mysteries of love and divine power which the soul itself cannot grasp and understand except in the light of Jesus. There it sees them with a splendour so great that they become sensible and in some sort palpable; but that light gone, the soul is lost in abysses, full of light, it is true, but in which it does not know and cannot know itself. It cannot, then, but be lost in wonder at the infinite wisdom of Jesus, His love, His mercy, which have made the priesthood so great. It cannot but be amazed and grieved to see how little the power of the priest, his sublime and truly divine dignity, are understood!

January 12, 1882. How great appears to me the thirst that Jesus in the Host has for the holiness of His ministers! In addition to this vision an interior voice earnestly presses me to pray much and sacrifice myself unceasingly in union with Jesus in the Host, to ask for the renewal of the sacerdotal spirit in the priests of Holy Church, and the religious spirit in souls consecrated to God. This voice seems to say that the weakening of this spirit is one of the wounds of the Church, the cause of bitter sorrows to the Heart of Jesus.

The interior light reveals to me in some way the depth of this wound and of this evil, showing me how the Church counts few priests who reach the standard of their sublime vocation, truly realising the greatness, the importance, of their sacred engagements.

Except a certain number who have remained faithful, some have become mercenaries, and become still more so every day; forgetting the care of the sheep which are confided to them, leaving them to be scattered and lost; neglecting to give them the bread to nourish them, the water to quench their thirst, the life and light to enlighten them.

The cause of this failure in the life of the priest is that he is not well filled with the spirit of detachment from the world, where he is placed by his great office of mediator between man and the Supreme Mediator, Jesus in the Blessed Sacrament.

Placed by that office between heaven and earth, the soul of a priest is like a sanctuary for the reconciliation of souls,—a sanctuary shut to all human things, open only to God and to souls; and as, in order to grasp these souls, it is necessary for him to come down to the earth on which they dwell, he must take care not to let the dust of the world stick to his feet.

Consecrated, given up to God and to souls by the very grace of his priesthood, the priest must save himself for these two great ends, to which his whole being belongs. He should stoop down to creatures only through love for what is divine in them, in order to make it grow and flourish; to catch hold of souls in order to raise and bring them to God should be his only work.

The light shows to me that these great duties which form the essence of the holy obligations of the priesthood, a principle of life or of death for souls, are not understood by some ministers of God; because they look only at the surface, and do not grasp their capital importance. They do not safeguard the sanctuary of their soul, but let in another spirit than that of God into the shrine, which the spirit of Jesus should fill with His fulness; when lo! the treasure-house is empty, where it should be full-laden with a store ever abounding, yet without losing any of its riches.

Self-seeking creeps in where divine action ought to do all, to work all; an ill-disguised selfishness takes the place of true zeal; the beauty of the home of Jesus and of souls is set at naught.

Such is the revelation of the light, before which I would not tarry through fear of being deceived or of exaggerating to myself an evil which I fear is immense—an evil which is shown to me as likely to be the cause and beginning of all other evils.

But grace was quick to render still stronger the conviction which the light impressed upon my soul as to the reality of these things.

To-day I was struck by the words of the third verse of Psalm lxxi. : *Suscipiant montes pacem*—" Let the mountains receive peace for the people, and the hills justice ". These words have been a new ray of light to my soul, making me understand the need of prayer for priests and for religious souls, and the great evil caused to the souls of the faithful by the neglect of the holy duties of these sublime vocations.

It seemed to me that the mountains which receive peace for the people are a figure of the souls of priests, who, by their holiness, ought to be like the mountains, rising between heaven and earth, upon which God rains down His peace, His blessings, His graces, to be poured forth by their means upon all souls. Less elevated than the mountains, the hills which receive justice seem to me to be the souls of religious, who, by their life of union with their Divine Spouse, their incessant sacrifices, their detachment from created things, ought to receive justice; that is, by their whole life to offer to God satisfaction to His divine justice for the sins of the world. The holiness of the soul of the priest and the perfection of the religious soul seem to me to be the channels by which grace and mercy descend upon the world—a rampart which breaks the darts of the justice of God. But if these channels are not such as to receive the grace and mercy, if the rampart is too weak to parry such assaults, it follows, of necessity, that souls pine and die away for want of help, or, again, are punished for their sins, having no one to protect and save them. I am terrified by the revelations of the light, and much more so by the light itself. If I do not realise in myself the perfection required by the graces which have been given me, I acknowledge myself worthy of all the chastisements of Jesus in the Host.

January 25, 1882. It is shown me that

to pray for the priest is to work in the most efficacious manner possible to hasten the advent of the reign of Jesus in the Blessed Sacrament. Holy Church, in confiding to him the guardianship of the Adorable Victim, has by this very fact made him the herald of the Eucharistic mysteries, of which he is both at the same time the faithful minister and happy witness. It is on the priest that God and the Church rely for the care and the guidance of souls through the shadows of faith to the hidden light, where God, who is more hidden still, is revealed. To pray for the priest seems to me to comfort Jesus again in His most bitter sorrows, and to give the sweetest consolations to His Sacred Heart; because, on account of the intimate friendship into which our Divine Saviour would enter with His ministers, on account of the sacred rights which He would have them exercise over His own Person, and of the entire and loving dependence He would have on them, it is by the priest that Jesus is either most afflicted or most consoled. In a word, to pray for the priest is, it seems to me, to rejoice the Holy Church of God, whose greatest consolation is her fruitfulness, and this fruitfulness cannot be hers except by the inviolable fidelity of her ministers to their sublime mission ; because she has consecrated them, and appointed them spiritual fathers of the children whom they are called to bring forth to her in Jesus, her Divine Spouse. In bestowing on the priest the sacred right of fatherhood over souls, the Church, at the same time, confides to him the key of the divine treasury, wherefrom to draw the food to nourish and support them, in order that they may bring forth fruit a hundredfold. Upon him, therefore, falls the duty of opening this divine treasury, of distributing its riches among souls, in order to give them life and light, to nourish them, to present them pure and stainless to their Immaculate Mother, by uniting them to the life of her Divine Spouse.

Chapter II.

THE ASSOCIATION OF THE PRIESTHOOD.

In the month of October, 1882, the Reverend Mother St. Teresa received from Our Lord the order to found an association of priests. On that undertaking she wrote down thoughts, from which a few extracts are made.*

November 22, 1882. My dear Lord Jesus said to me about the "Association of the Priesthood": "My daughter, I want prudence: it is necessary; but especially and above all do I want self-surrender and confidence. I wish to do this work alone; and I alone have chosen and marked with the seal of My love and of My mercy the souls that are to be its members. . . . My daughter, souls have been made for the Association, it is true, but it is the Association above all which has been formed for souls, and which will make them worthy of it and fit to do its service.

* The Rules of this Association are to be found in her life, Vol. II., pp. 176-192.

"In becoming members of this body souls will catch its spirit, and by receiving the graces which are its privilege will be made worthy of it. Would it not be folly to expect a wild plant to produce the fruits of a good tree, before being engrafted in it and nourished with its sap? To require souls to have its spirit and fully understand it before becoming members would be unreasonable.

"As the wild plant should be of a nature disposed to receive the sap which is to take the place of its own bitter juices, to give it the properties of the tree which is to quicken it and to make it bear its fruits, so must the souls called to *the Association* possess in themselves dispositions and aptitudes to receive the spirit and the graces of this work. I, having predestined these souls, have given them these dispositions, these aptitudes, which are in those souls as germs, which will grow as soon as the spirit and the graces of the work shall be gained by them."

After speaking thus to me, Jesus rested me upon His Heart; and I immediately felt mine impressed with the ardent desire which filled His Eucharistic Heart to see His work flourish and produce its fruits.

But I understood that this full development would not take place until souls should have been regenerated by the fire of tribulation.

Showing me how great should be this tribulation, Jesus said to me:

"The time of My justice is come; I have already arisen, and am coming to avenge My immaculate spouse for the outrages which she has suffered from unnatural children; I will cast back upon those, who ought to be her glory and her crown, the shame and ignominy with which they have covered her. But before executing My vengeance, I will lay the foundation of My work in souls whom My love shall safe-guard. Hidden during the storm, but surely protected, these foundations shall then be seen, and upon them I will build My living house."

The thought of the chastisement had frozen me with fear; but that of the good for souls that Jesus was to draw from it, and the glory He would gain, gave me strength to desire the trial which would prepare the way for the reign of the Eucharistic Heart, and give to Jesus the victory.

December 22, 1882. My dearest Saviour deigned to show me that the rules of the "Association of the Priesthood" are after His own Heart, are its living expression, and that in them is to be found the remedy for the harm which spreads among souls from the priest, and wounds them unto death.

In my contemplation I heard Jesus speak these words: "Every priestly soul, bearing in itself the Sun of Justice, ought to give back His divine rays. Light of the world of souls, his mission is to enlighten them by displaying Me to them, shining before their eyes in divine perfections, so that they may perceive the divine mysteries which are in Me, and which are beyond the reach of their feeble sight.

"As in the time of My mortal life My Sacred Manhood was for men the visible Sacrament of the Godhead, and as it was by it that the Word spoke to souls and illuminated them with His divine splendour, eclipsed under the veils of the flesh, so, in My mystical and sacramental life among men, the priest is My visible Sacrament: it is by him that I speak to souls, and by the grace of the Holy Spirit accompanying his exterior word that I enlighten them and give them the knowledge of My exterior mysteries. Replenished with My God-like splendour, the soul of the priest becomes the lamp of souls. But as every lamp combines both light and heat, the priest must unite in himself the body and the soul of the sacred science; that is to say, his holiness must be fed by his doctrine, and his doctrine quickened by his holiness; so that, by means of both, he may penetrate into the innermost of My mysteries, to gather from them the spirit and the grace that he is to impart to souls."

. . . .

Showing me the state of a certain number of consecrated souls, Jesus said to me: "They have but vestiges of My Spirit left in them. The world has entered into them, with all its blindness, its cupidity, its desires, its corruption; these sanctuaries are nothing but temples of idols, wherein incense is lavished before all sorts of divinities. How could My Spirit dwell in places so profaned? Pray, My daughter, pray for these souls, who are only stumbling-blocks to those whom they ought to save."

These words broke my heart, and but for the foresight Jesus gave me of the consolation He would receive from the "Association of the Priesthood," I could not have endured the pain I felt.

An interior light revealed to me the signification of these words of Jesus: "The world . . . with its *blindness*," &c. I saw that by *blindness* Jesus meant to speak of the weakness of the understanding of those priests who, living as those that are of the earth earthy, cannot rise to the pure regions of faith to be enlightened with the brightness of Eternal Truth.

By *cupidity* my dearest Saviour would point out the love of luxury and of riches, which render these souls slaves of matter; souls who ought to be completely detached, so as to reflect the poverty of Jesus, and to live for the good of all, especially of the little ones and of the needy.

By *desires* Jesus meant that unquenchable thirst after honours, dignities, and applause, which desire, being without merit, and therefore without virtue, without reverence for God, leads these souls to sue for whatever position they desire to occupy. I cannot describe all the sufferings of Jesus from such upstarts of human protection and favour, and all the prejudice caused to souls.

By *corruption* Jesus signified the weakening of the Spirit of Christ in such souls; and, as that Spirit quickens, animates, and perfects all things, when it fails, whether totally or in part, everything becomes impaired, tainted, and ends in corruption, just in proportion as the action of this quickening Spirit is required.

Jesus showed me, on the other hand, the divine authority with which the priesthood is invested, and its lofty mission in the Church. He said to me: " The priest is the Sacrament of God among men; he is Christ living in the Church; he ought thus to be the father of the poor, the help of the weak, the staff of the infirm, the light of the blind, the comforter of the afflicted, the guide of those who go astray. All this he is in Me, or rather I am all this in him, when it is I only who live in his soul."

. . . .

. . . *1883.* This morning my dearest Lord urged me to pray for the " Association of the Priesthood," which I did during Mass and after Communion. I had no special inspiration, except that I saw the most loving and supremely lovable Heart of Jesus-Priest grievously wounded, unworthily outraged by the souls of priests who do not live the life of Christ, who do not act according to His Spirit.

Whilst considering this vision, I thought I heard Jesus say to me :

" Making reparation cannot heal the wound, which the sons of My love have inflicted on My Heart ; it must be *a corrective* of the evil that causes it ".

I had a vision then of the " Association of the Priesthood," and, in continuing to pray for it, I felt that I comforted Jesus more efficaciously than by making amends for the injuries which He had received from consecrated souls.

Showing me the souls of the Eucharistic Association of the Priesthood, Jesus added:

"I would have each of them to be a living fire of love, that all these fires together might make a blazing furnace in which My Heart, by a new exercise of My love, should melt the hearts of iron which resist the ordinary action of My grace".

. . . *1883.* This morning my dearest Lord showed me the "Association of the Priesthood," with all the difficulties it would have to overcome, to be established, to be what Jesus wishes it to be. These difficulties were so great, that, humanly speaking, the work seemed to me almost impossible; but Jesus, who showed me this human impossibility, said to me: "It is a small matter to My omnipotence, which is never better seen than in nothingness. Did I not say that I alone would found this Association, and that, having done so, none of the instruments employed by Me shall be able to say: This is my work. I would have all contribute to it by self-sacrifice, by annihilation of self, in order to offer a living and perpetual holocaust to Me, as Priest of God My Father, and to My Eternal Priesthood.

. . . .

"By this Association I would rebuild the ruins of My Church. By Myself alone can I work this miracle. To do so I only ask for docile, pure, and simple souls. My love shall be manifest in the choice of the means that I shall employ to rebuild My city, and My omnipotence will be shown in the work, which I shall accomplish Myself together with man, but without the help of man.

. . . .

"It is not strength I need but love, that love which begets true zeal; weakness in obedience to Me is far more powerful than strength, which would work in and by itself. I desire therefore only a devoted love, a weakness of obedience.

. . . .

"I call for souls whom I sign with the seal of My love, so that, guided by this same love, acting in the unity of My spirit, they may unite their efforts and work together, each according to its own weak means, for the building up of the Church and the conversion of souls."

While I rested upon His Heart, my dearest Lord Jesus revealed Himself to me, as the Glorifier of God His Father, as His living praise. Showing to me His Sacred Heart, as the Holy Temple wherefrom rises this divine praise adequate to the infinite perfections it celebrates: showing to me also the souls of priests as the holy instruments by which His Divine Heart raises His glorifying voice to the throne of the Trinity, Jesus said to me: " I am the substantial praise of the Church, and I am therein always glorifying My Father. But this praise has not always its living echoes.

" Among souls that I have made for praise, there are some who have forgotten how to pour forth praise; I am about to avenge the shame with which they are covering Me, by keeping My praise and My word in prison. I shall glorify My Father in them, but it will be by justice and not by love, as My Heart would have it.

"I am forming souls for a new praise, for I will not have My Spouse covered any longer with confusion by ungrateful sons. These souls will praise Me in spirit and in truth; they will continue the glory which I give to God My Father."

By these words Jesus showed to me that He would not cease to render to God His Father a twofold praise, a twofold glory, one all from within, in His holy soul, in His Sacred Heart, by the adoration, the contemplation of the perfections towards which He always looks, which He is always contemplating in themselves, which He adores and loves for themselves; the other from without, by the entire devotedness, the unceasing sacrifice of all His Sacred Manhood, to make men know' and love God His Father; and to offer to this most Holy Father a tribute of perpetual homage and loving servitude.

I saw that this twofold praise forms the essence of the worship that Jesus renders to the Holy Trinity, and that the need, the desire of His Heart is to continue it in souls, and to render it through them. I understood that our Divine Saviour wishes to satisfy His desire in the association of the Blessed Sacrament and of the Priesthood. Showing me that these two works made only one, as these two praises form but one and the same praise, Jesus said: "In and by Eucharistic souls I wish to continue My interior adoration, the praise of My Sacred Soul; and as it is only in Me and by Me that they will be true adorers and glorifiers of the Father, and as I shall be Myself the praise and the adoration, I would have them always contemplating Me as I Myself contemplate the Father and His divine perfections for themselves. I wish them to have towards Me not a regard of feeling and sentiment, but a love arising from the will and from the intelligence, that they may see My virtues in themselves, and make them live in them.

"Like unto the seraphim of God, who are consumed by the fire of love in the adoration of the Divine Essence, and are transformed in God by this adoration, the Eucharistic souls, the seraphim of My Sacred Manhood, by their office shall be transformed in Me by turning their whole being towards My Heart in the Host; and as God, by reflecting His infinite perfections in the seraphim, is to Himself His own praise and His glory, so My virtues, passing into Eucharistic souls, shall be fitting praise and glory to My Heart.

"The souls of priests ought to be the instruments of My external praise. Being the living tongue of My holy Spouse and My own voice, they ought to publish My praise so as to be heard by all.

"As the cherubim who surround the throne of the Eternal receive His Godlike splendour and reflect it upon the other hierarchies, thus My priests ought to reflect My virtues, and make them shine in souls; they publish thus My praise, and are My glory. But their voices, whose words ought to be heard to the ends of the world, are dumb, and only utter sounds which cannot be heard nor understood.

"To these souls I am forming I shall give

a voice which shall be heard above the murmurs of those who have no longer any voice to praise Me; they shall be to Me pure victims—victims of loudest praise; by them My voice will ascend to My Father, and will be heard by souls."

My dearest Lord showed me how His Eucharistic Heart rejoices and rests in the glory which the Association is to render Him.

It seemed that I heard Him say to me: "In My divine foreknowledge I see this glory, and, as all time is present to Me, I welcome it already, to quell the cry of blasphemy that some consecrated souls have uttered against Me and against My Father".

While hearing these words, I saw that this cry of blasphemy is but the natural life of these priests and religious women, who, by the opposition they make to the life of Jesus, cast upon Jesus Himself shame and ignominy, and expose Him in the persons of these souls to the raillery, sarcasms, and derision of the world.

Jesus, again addressing me, said: "My daughter, already am I glorifying Myself in the souls of the Association, for in them I see the will of My Father accomplished. I am rendering thanks for the great glory gained by God from them through Me. Know well that the greatest, the only glory the creature can give to God is to live in itself the life which the Holy Trinity had planned for it from all eternity."

I was struck this morning by these words of Jesus: "I am preparing a peaceful army, which is to vanquish the spirit of darkness; by it My truth shall be victorious over lies, My love shall triumph over hatred. The lamp which I am preparing for My Christ is already lit. I am making its light more brilliant, and am preparing the reign of love, of light, of truth."

I understood that the peaceful army of which Jesus spoke was the Association, and that the lamp of Christ was the souls of this work, revealing Jesus to the world, and revealing Him to it as light and love.

www.ingramcontent.com/pod-product-compliance
Lightning Source LLC
Chambersburg PA
CBHW030345170426
43202CB00010B/1245